Write It to Win It! 39 Secrets from a Screenwriting Contest Judge

Write It to Win It! 39 Secrets from a Screenwriting Contest Judge

Sean Hinchey

Foreword by Christopher Lockhart

Havenhurst Books
Los Angeles

Havenhurst Books, Los Angeles 90046
© 2011 Havenhurst Books
All rights reserved. Published 2011
Printed in the United States of America
14 13 12 11 10 09 5 4 3 2 1
ISBN 978-0-9822853-6-7   0-9822853-6-1
Hinchey, Sean
Write It to Win It! 39 Secrets from a Screenwriting Contest Judge

Cover Design: Leo Baligaya
Interior Design: Leo Baligaya

To Lana and Isley, the two most wonderful girls in my life

TABLE OF CONTENTS

FOREWORD: THE ROAD TO HOLLYWOOD — ix
by Christopher Lockhart

ONE: INTRODUCTION — 1
Who am I? — 1
The Process — 3
How to Drive This Book — 8
Key Points — 12

TWO: PREPARATION — 13
Are You Ready to Win? — 13
Formatting — 18
Script Packaging — 23
Page Count — 27
Pitching — 31
Key Points — 36

THREE: PRESENTATION AND PRECAUTIONS — 37
Text & Style — 37
Description — 41
Dialogue — 47
Watch Your Tone — 55
Voice-over — 61
Flashbacks — 67
Key Points — 71

FOUR: STRUCTURE — 72
The Want — 72
Conflict — 78
Act I: Great Openings — 82
Act II: The Vast Desert — 86
Significant Details — 93
Act III: Great Endings — 96
Key Points — 102

FIVE: CHARACTERS — 104
Defining Your Protagonist — 104
The Anti-Hero — 109
Creating Your Villain — 114
Secondary Characters — 121
Casting — 126
Key Points — 130

SIX: GENRES — 131
Genre & Theme — 131
Drama — 135
Comedy — 138
Science Fiction (Sci-Fi) — 142
Horror — 146
Period Piece — 152
Westerns — 156
Thriller — 160
Family — 165
Non-Linear — 168
High Concept — 174
Key Points — 180

SEVEN: DETAILS — 182
A Great Title — 182
Iconic Moment — 185
The Notes Will Tell Me Why I Lost — 190
Repetition is Redundant — 193
Avoid the Ordinary — 196
Key Points — 202

EIGHT: THE BIG QUESTION — 203
Can Your Script Be Produced? — 203

ACKNOWLEDGMENTS — 208
SUGGESTED READING & RESOURCES — 209
ABOUT THE AUTHOR — 212

FOREWORD: THE ROAD TO HOLLYWOOD

The road to Hollywood is neither a sprint nor a marathon. It's a death march.

It's often a long and grueling journey that prevents most people from ever arriving. The dream of the actor landing a big role, the writer selling her script, the director helming a critically-acclaimed film or a producer seeing his vision come to fruition eludes almost everyone who tries. The birth of the Internet, programs like Final Draft, and the explosion of digital media have created a proliferation of content that far exceeds the needs of the entertainment industry to rarely fulfills its expectations.

The aspiring screenwriter has it particularly tough because his audition amounts to 120 pages of screenplay that can cost an executive two hours out of his weekend. An actor, in comparison, has a two-minute reel and a headshot that tells the executive what he needs to know with much less of a time investment. And with Hollywood drowning in screenplays, how does a new writer capture the attention of a busy producer or executive?

Screenwriting contests, though hardly a new invention, have become a popular way to try to access the film industry. While many contests are useless in their ability to provide entrée, a few have been quite effective in introducing writers with no previous contacts to executives, agents, managers, and producers. Winning a respected screenwriting contest (like the Nicholl Fellowship in Screenwriting, for example) can create "heat" around a screenplay and even pave the way to a script sale and subsequent production. Careers have been launched from screenwriting contests. Even without all the pomp and circumstance, contests force writers to set goals, add extra excitement to the writing process, and maybe provide some bragging rights.

When Sean Hinchey asked me to read his new book *Write It to Win It! 39 Secrets from a Screenwriting Contest Judge*, the idea sounded like overkill. 39 secrets? There's just <u>one</u> secret to winning a screenwriting contest. And it's not even much of a secret: Just write a great script! But after a pause, I realized that kind of advice is rather vague and flippant. What does "great" mean? What powerful dramatic elements exist in a great screenplay that allows it to rise above all other competitors to be called the best?

Write It to Win It! talks about those very elements that create a memorable piece of dramatic writing, but it also offers a rare inside look at the thought process of those who judge material. As a result, this becomes an indispensable and potent guide to writing that winning screenplay.

While most authors write a script with an actor or director or agent in mind, few write with the reader in mind. The one common denominator between the actor, director, and agent is that they are all readers. Since the first hurdle for any writer is to get past the reader, it's imperative to consider how the experience will be perceived during that intimate exchange between screenplay and reader.

Mr. Hinchey's delivery is sometimes a bit harsh and always uncompromising, which is exactly the way material is vetted behind closed doors at studios and agencies. The industry doesn't have time to teach because it's busy making movies. It expects the writer to arrive prepared. This book offers that preparation: the critical thinking, the strategies and the thought processes that go into writing and evaluating material, whether the goal is to win a screenwriting contest or land an agent, and it uses lots of examples from popular films to illustrate its points.

Doesn't it make sense to think like the person who passes judgment on your material?

Write It to Win It! can help put the writer and her screenplay on a straight path to Hollywood, making that arduous journey a lot less painful. Good luck in your creative endeavors, and I look forward to seeing your name in the trade papers announcing that big win in a screenwriting contest.

Christopher Lockhart
Beverly Hills, California

Christopher Lockhart is a film executive, educator, and producer. He is the Story Editor at WME, the world's biggest talent agency, where he looks for projects for clients including Denzel Washington and Steve Martin. He has an MFA in dramatic writing from NYU and lectures around the country. His writing workshop "The Inside Pitch" was produced for television and earned him an LA Area Emmy nomination. He co-produced *The Collector* (2009) and its sequel, *The Collection* (2012). He wrote and produced the documentary *Most Valuable Players* (2010), which won the Documentary Channel Audience Award at the 2011 Nashville Film Festival and was acquired by Oprah Winfrey as part of the OWN *Documentary Club*. He has been a guest judge for screenwriting contests like *Big Break Contest!*, *The Wisconsin Screenwriting Contest* and the UCLA Showcase 2011. He is a member of the Academy of Television Arts and Sciences, The Writers Guild of America, West and the Producers Guild of America.

ONE: INTRODUCTION

WHO AM I?

The first logical question that anyone would likely ask of somebody writing a book such as this is, who is this guy?

I've been a Script Reader for International Creative Management (ICM), Miracle Entertainment, Nash Entertainment, Viviano Entertainment and Scr(i)pt Magazine. I've read the preliminary drafts of Michael Crichton's best-selling novels, *State of Fear* and *Next* and have performed extensive research for the stage plays and screenplays of writer/director Floyd Mutrux know for *American Me* (1992), *Mulholland Falls* (1996) and *Million Dollar Quartet* (2009).

I'm an active consultant for screenplays and books and I judge for many prestigious screenwriting contests, including *Big Break, Artists' and Writers' Contest, Smart Contest,* and *Chills and Thrills Contest*. During that time, I've read over *three thousand* screenplays.

But this doesn't give you the full picture of what I know.

Let me put that amount of reading into context for you. Most scripts are between ninety and one hundred and twenty pages. We'll say that on average all of the scripts that I've read are one hundred pages. Again, some are more, some are less, but one hundred pages falls somewhere in the middle. That equals *three hundred thousand* pages of written material. If you were to tape all the pages together and roll it out, you would have a ribbon of paper *fifty-two miles* long! Can you imagine crawling on your hands and knees for that distance, while reading?

Sean Hinchey

This figure doesn't even include the dozens of books I've consulted on.

I wrote and produced *Dirty Bomb Diaries (DBD)* a 16-episode web-series that was made for $600, and reached 2 Million internet hits. The video is appearing on a variety of sites, including TubeFilter.tv, KoldCast.tv, StayTunedTV.net and Strike.tv. and has been the subject of many interviews.

Three of my screenplays have been optioned and one was a finalist in the "Film in Arizona Screenwriting Competition." My first non-fiction book, *Backpacking Through Divorce* won a "Fresh Voices" award.

This book is a culmination of these experiences, and I am very happy to share them with you, so that you may win a screenwriting competition!

THE PROCESS

Put a script before me and I transform into the reader, the judge, and the gatekeeper. I am what stands between you and the reality of winning a screenplay contest. As a judge, I decide if your name will be smattered across a full-page ad in Variety magazine. Unlike some sour-faced doorman sporting sun glasses and a strange haircut I want to unclip the red velvet rope and let you into the club. I am on your side.

But never, ever, ever waste my time, or your work will get thrown into a bottomless recycling bin.

My wrath means a silent defeat for you, because you didn't follow a few simple rules. Rules that help me choose your material out of the endless sea of screenplays that overwhelm the Hollywood screenwriting contest scene.

To understand my harsh, detached approach to reading a screenplay you need to realize how the process works. Do I soak in a hot bath and eat chocolates while I gaze in wonderment at the script cradled in my hands? Do I take my time, reading each script over the course of several days? Do I re-read your script to make sure that I've understood every nuance, every arc, and every setback? No.

I treat it like a job. I hunker down, and I read… and read… and read. I am being paid to find the top scripts out of the hundreds of stories that I have to sort through. You need to realize that I am tasked with reading for a contest, not writing coverage reports. Very big difference. You are competing, not seeking feedback. There are no names or addresses, sometimes there isn't even a title. Nothing to skew my judgment. Just a script that requires a cold, logical appraisal by myself and other judges like me.

While I do read the entire script and follow it up with a brief contest coverage report, I have a general idea of how good your writing is early on. Here's how I work. I pick up each script, and read the first ten pages. Here's what I'm looking for: What is the story about? Who is the main character? What is the genre?

Think of it as a used car lot. One car looks good from a distance. Close up, there are dings in the hood, another car has a flat tire, and several of them have smashed windshields. There are so many more intact vehicles for me to choose from.

How is your description? Too much prose? A fifteen-line paragraph of wordy redundancy? Yes, I've read scripts where the first five pages are non-stop blocks of dense text. Great for a novel, bad for scripts. If this happens, my mind will begin to shut down.

Any script that comes in under ninety pages or is over one hundred and thirty will also be flagged. Additions, such as a synopsis, cast list with a character bio, budget breakdown always scream out, "Amateur!"

Why am I so harsh? Because I have so many scripts to plow through. It doesn't matter if the script gets better after page twenty, because I know I will find several scripts that will grab me from page one. Nevertheless, I continue flipping through the script as I read sections of dialogue. Are people actually talking, or just exchanging pleasantries? I pick two scenes at random to read all the way through.

What I am doing is sampling. Do the scenes seem

complete? Does something happen or is it just filler? Is the description crisp and to the point? Does the dialogue flow? Am I engaged in this screenplay? At this point, I don't care as much about the story as I do about your knowledge of the craft. Can you write? Now that I am familiar with your material, I begin reading it from page one.

Do you have a problem with my process? Then let me ask this question of you. How do you select a book at a bookstore or library? The majority of people examine the cover, then flip to the back cover of the book to read the testimonials. Then it's on to the Table of Contents, perhaps a quick perusal of the foreword then you may skim a couple of chapters. Maybe you read the first paragraph of several chapters before you either put it back on the shelf, or tuck it under your arm.

You are trying to familiarize yourself with the material before you make a decision to read that book. For me, the process of flipping through a screenplay is also a way to clear my head of the last script. It's like a mental sorbet that prepares me for the next screenplay I'm about to dive into.

As I get into the reading process, I may go through a dozen, or even two dozen scripts that have no chance of making it further in the contest. But then I find that one script that has something which grabs my attention. Plenty of white space, catchy dialogue, concise descriptions, and an appealing premise that slowly reveals itself. These are the writers that trust that I know how to read a script. Nothing is rammed down my throat. This script makes it into my finalist pile!

What happens if I'm on the fence with a script? Let's say

the dialogue is good, but I'm not sure that you've taken the story to its logical end. Great premise, but who are these characters? If you've managed to get my brain in a knot, and have me questioning if I like it or not, then I'm giving you the benefit of the doubt. It goes to the next round because you've gotten your script stuck in my head.

When it's all said and done, maybe 3-5% of all scripts will make it to the next round. How can I cull a pile of screenplays down to such a small stack of potential winners?

Easy. I know what I'm doing.

Malcolm Gladwell, a *New Yorker* magazine regular, wrote *Blink (2005)* where he talks about people's ability to understand something almost instantaneously. As an example, he discusses the Getty Museum's purchase of an ancient Greek statue that had all of the proper documentation to prove it was authentic. However, a group of experts immediately knew something was amiss: the find of the century was a forgery.

The crux of his book is that people who are properly trained in their respective niche can assess the information and make the correct call in the blink of an eye. While they may not be able to explain how they can do it, they can feel that their decision is correct. It's more than just intuition. Their skills become second nature.

Perhaps some of you are salespeople. You just know when a deal is going to close in the first couple minutes of a meeting. On a first date, you have an idea immediately if there is a chance that the relationship will go anywhere. There are people involved in fantasy football leagues who never seem to lose. It's not luck, it's a special knack that they have.

You may disagree with my method of picking a winner. But, this is my system. I've picked scripts from the first round out of hundreds of scripts that have gone on to win the top prize. I've selected screenplays that have not only made it to the finalist round, but have gone on to win in another screenwriting contest. You may think it's unfair that I take an enormous amount of scripts and reduce them down to a mere handful. However, that is what I am paid to do. Yes, it's a subjective opinion, but there can only be one winner, and somebody has to trim the stack. I immerse myself in the process, and I've been doing it for a long time.

Because of that, I'm being hired to find the diamond in the rough, and from that cold, callous point of view I don't give a damn if you win or not. I work for the contest not the writer. But don't worry, because I've been pulling for you since day one. Even though I'm not emotionally involved in your success or loss, I don't want to spend all that time reading bad scripts. I want to enjoy myself. *I want to read a great script.* That's why I'm here.

Do you think the judges of *American Idol* sit at their table because they want to listen to bad singers? No, they want all the contestants to be great. Sometimes a judge gets irritated at the competitor who thinks they should be a star but don't have a shred of talent. Why? Because the bad contestants are taking valuable time away from the artists who can actually sing.

When any judge opens the first page of your script, they want that script to be the winner. They are on your side, you have their attention. Dazzle them.

Sean Hinchey

HOW TO DRIVE THIS BOOK

The idea for this book is based upon my personal notes from reading thousands of scripts over the years. I would read one script for a contest and find several mistakes that, if corrected, would have drastically increased its chances of winning. Instead, I'd drop the screenplay into the recycle bin and move on.

Over time, I accumulated more and more notes on what makes a screenplay fail. It's easy to critique a good script; you know it when you see it. Trying to understand why a poorly written script doesn't deliver the goods can be hard to explain. That is what this book is about, allowing the writer to recognize when their screenplay isn't working as well as it could. Then, giving them the information needed to make it better.

You may be able to recognize some, or all, of these secrets as actual flaws in your own script. You may make the corrections and enter a screenwriting contest. Still, there is no guarantee that you will win. You may ignore every single one of these secrets, enter your script into the next contest and win the top prize. Anything is possible.

The reality is, the majority of people who read this book will never even make it to the finalist round in a screenwriting contest. This is just a cold, hard fact. My goal is not to give anyone false hope, or even imply a guarantee that by reading this book you will win.

My desire is that these secrets will give the serious writer an advantage. I'm talking about the guy who gives up partying with friends on a Friday night to hammer out a scene; the woman who stays up until the wee hours rewriting and goes into work bleary-eyed. These are the writers who silently toil away, honing their craft into something they believe in. All of this in the hopes that their work wins a screenwriting contest and opens doors to possibilities beyond their imagination.

It has happened for some people, and it will happen again.

If you're still reading this far, then you want to try your hand at writing what could be a contest-winning script. If you're willing to give it your best shot, then I will clearly and concisely give you all the gems that I've learned so you can make it happen. This book is about *your* journey, I'm just along for the ride.

Here's how this book works. The chapters are broken down into individual sections. I will reference a great number of films throughout the book. I urge you to not get sidetracked by trying to figure out if they are a favorite film for either of us. This book isn't about critiquing movies. They are just used as examples.

If you find that a certain chapter doesn't pertain to you, then feel free to skip ahead. However, you may miss some information that could come into play later in the book. I've purposely crafted the sections to be bite-sized. I recognize that the majority of us have regular jobs, family obligations and the need to make time to write. Read it at your leisure.

Some points I use in the book may seem redundant in later chapters. Because there are so many different facets to writing, I may approach the same subject matter from various angles. Although the subject may be similar, the manner in which I discuss it is different.

Also, you may find that some of the sections don't have many movie references. The reason is that I am coming from the perspective of a contest judge. The majority of the problems that contest-submitted scripts suffer from, would get ironed out in successive drafts by more than one writer on any given project. If you see two writers on the credits for a movie, there's probably four more uncredited writers behind them; they are called "script doctors." But that's a subject for a whole different book.

Keep in mind that each point I make won't necessarily make or break your script if you ignore my suggestions. But, an error here or a bit of sloppiness there can add up quickly. It's like downhill skiing in the Olympics. The difference between the gold medal and last place can be mere thousandths of a second. That could've been caused by a ski pole that wasn't tight to the body, or a crouch in a turn that wasn't perfectly aerodynamic.

Same goes for screenwriting contests. Everyone is being judged by the material they submit. While yours may be good, if the next script I read is crafted just a little bit better, yours will get bumped down a notch. The secrets that I'm sharing with you would shave entire seconds off the clock, if writing were an Olympic ski event. I am going to present you with writing errors that you may have never thought of.

I've attempted to put the book together in a logical and orderly manner. The chapters toward the back of the book are just as important as the earlier ones and each chapter has different lengths from other ones. The individual page count for each section shouldn't be used to gauge what is important and what isn't. This goes back to recognizing that you would be better suited working on your script than reading redundant passages in this book. When I make my point, I move on.

As you read the book, I use the terms "judge," "audience," and "reader" interchangeably. They are all correct in the context of this book because no matter how you write your script, at some point you are going to have to dazzle at least one of these entities.

While I will do my best to explain everything that I know in great detail, there is something that you will need to bring to the table as the reader of this book. Whatever is said here shouldn't be taken personally by you. You will need to detach yourself from your screenplay. It's now a product to be modified, altered and shared with the world.

My approach may seem harsh, indifferent, or uncaring. For the most part, it is. However, my intent is not to be insulting or belittling. I do understand the time commitment it takes to write a script. I've written dozens of them over the years in addition to this book. You need to realize that people in the film industry see thousands, if not, tens of thousands of scripts flowing past their desks every year. It's a business, they treat it like one, so should you. If you're looking for an ego stroke, go elsewhere. The best writers are the people who can take criticism in stride. They are detached, because they want to succeed. If you can take that approach to your writing, you are above and beyond the other writers trying to break into the film industry.

Continuing on with the setup for this book would be futile. Time is precious, so let's get down to business.

KEY POINTS

- Understand that the contest reading process is a brutal assessment of your material, not of you as a person.

- Selling a script and winning a contest are against the odds; your writing has to be great across the board.

- Don't get angry at the judges, or the process, if you don't win a contest. Picking a winner is subjective.

- While you may feel that not every chapter or section in this book applies to your writing, you may just learn something valuable if you read the whole book.

- Examples from movies are meant to be used only as examples, not as a critiques of the films.

- Your screenplay is a product, so detach yourself from it so that you don't take any analysis of it personally.

TWO: PREPARATION

ARE YOU READY TO WIN?

Before you can thrust yourself fully into writing an award-winning screenplay, you need to ask yourself one question: Are you prepared to win? This may sound as though you are getting ahead of yourself. As this book progresses, you will be not only better prepared to win a script contest, but to get out there and sell your script.

There are **Two Angles** to this question that will be explored which will help you on your writing journey.

First, what does winning a screenwriting contest actually mean?

For the moment, let's pretend that you've received a phone call announcing that you are one of five finalists for a contest. Your first reaction will most likely be disbelief, then joy and happiness. You'll want to relish in the moment.

What will happen next is that you'll be invited to an event where the other finalists will also be in attendance. There may be a guest speaker, usually an A-List writer, and they'll be granted an honorary award for showing up. Then comes the moment you've been waiting for: the top scripts in the entire contest comes down to one shining moment.

The envelope is opened and your name is announced. Your photo is taken, you give a speech, shake a lot of people's hands and your name ends up in the trade newspapers. The next morning, you wake up and can't believe it happened. Is that all there is to it?

Sean Hinchey

Absolutely not!

This is where you need to be prepared to win the contest. Your goal should *not* be to win a screenwriting contest. That may throw you for a loop. Why are you reading this book then? What should be your ultimate goal?

It's to sell your screenplay to a production company that will make it into a movie.

When I point this out to writers who are focused on entering a screenwriting contest, they nod their heads vigorously and exclaim, "Well, of course I want to get my screenplay sold."

The only way to go about this writing process is to be consciously aware that the end game is the sale of your script. The contest needs to be a stepping stone on that path. If you ask any football player what their goal is, it's to win the Super Bowl. In order for them to do that, they need to focus on each and every game that they play. The more games they win, the closer they get to the prize.

After you win the contest, you will have an opportunity to meet with different production companies, agents, and managers. The key here is to strike while you are hot. Hollywood is very fickle and people are attracted to the next shiny object bobbing in front of them. Attention spans can be shorter than this sentence.

When you meet with these people, there are few things that will happen. You will go into an office, or maybe meet in a restaurant where this person, let's say they are an agent, will congratulate you on your win and tell you how wonderful your screenplay is. Chances are, they haven't even read it. Perhaps someone else in their office has and they gave the agent a synopsis.

At this point, it's not important if they've read your material. They are taking time out of their day to meet with you. What you are doing with this short period of time is selling yourself. Don't push the script.

Your contest-winning screenplay is a calling card, a flag that grabbed their attention. There is a distinct possibility that your screenplay doesn't appeal to them. It could be the genre, budget, or a variety of other reasons why your script isn't a good fit. You may be perfect for them, however. Perhaps they have a project that can take advantage of your talents. In case you missed it: Use this time to sell yourself.

The biggest mistake writers make when taking a meeting is that they close the door on themselves. For example, an agent will ask you what else you are working on. I've talked to many writers who are constantly rewriting and reworking their script and they haven't taken time to develop a new concept. If you tell the agent, "I don't have anything else right now," you've ended the conversation before the appetizers have arrived. Be prepared with one or two ideas, even if you haven't put anything down on paper.

Before your meeting, take some time to flesh out these ideas so you can discuss them at length. You want to show the agent that the script that won the contest isn't a flash in the pan. You are a person of substance; you can generate other screenplays of the same caliber.

You should be able to pitch these concepts, as well as give them the equivalent of a one paragraph synopsis, told in a conversational manner. They'll ask you questions about the story, maybe even offer some suggestions to improve it. Take it all in stride, it's just conversation.

When you two eventually do discuss your contest-winning screenplay, they may ask you if you've ever considered altering your material. For example, if you wrote a comedy that had characters in their mid-thirties, they may ask if you would consider changing your screenplay to a high school comedy.

If you immediately say "No!" you've once again ended the conversation. What you want to do is keep the discussion going. Bounce some ideas back and forth, you're not committing to anything. Keep in mind that what you think both of you are talking about isn't really what the exchange is about.

An agent may throw you some curve balls to see how you respond. Do you take offense easily at any suggestions regarding your material? Are you able to take in ideas and rationally discuss them? Do you have ideas for other projects?

What the agent wants to know is, are you an easy person to work with? If every suggestion on their part brings about drama on your part, then it won't be a good working relationship. Years are spent developing a script from words on paper to the big screen. Nobody wants to have an uphill battle the entire way.

The smart writer walks out of any meeting with a friendly handshake and a business card in hand to discuss any further projects. Even if the person you met with doesn't have anything for you, they may pass your name onto another person. When your name comes up in conversation, you want people's eyes to light up. You don't want the "Oh THAT person!" response, followed by an eye roll.

The second angle you want to be working on, while you are writing your screenplay is to build relationships on your own. Everything that was just discussed in this chapter is completely relevant even if you don't win a screenwriting contest.

Make calls to production companies, get people to read your script, and create connections through your own work. Always be developing a new idea. You may generate interest with a producer because of one script, even if the genre is all wrong. Six months later, you may present that same person with another screenplay that you've completed which is a fit for them.

Give out the vibe that you are easy to work with. This doesn't mean making each and every change to your screenplay that is suggested. People often times come up with ludicrous changes to a screenplay, that come off the top of their head. It's all chit chat, a collaborative brainstorm. People in Hollywood think aloud.

Let the conversations move forward regardless. If you should ink a deal, which has been your goal all along, then you can take a more serious approach to any suggestions that have been made. Until then, keep your eyes on the prize, move forward, and don't stop writing.

FORMATTING

I know: too basic, right? But in Hollywood, looks count. Before you even begin to write your script, make sure that you understand the rules regarding formatting of your screenplay. While this may sound like a minor detail, it actually can be the difference between winning a screenwriting contest or getting your script tossed into the recycle bin. First, we'll talk about the rules, then we'll discuss why they are so important.

All scripts should be written in Courier, 12-point font on 8.5" x 11" paper. Keep the left and right margins in the area of 1.5" and 1.0," respectively. As a contest judge, I implore you not to deviate from this rule.

The scene heading, or slug line, should be in ALL CAPS. It's important to keep the description sparse. Just tell us where you are and the portion of the day.

INT. CUBICLE OFFICE SPACE - EVENING

With description, the text will go from margin to margin. Go easy on italicized words or boldface in this part of your script. The first time you introduce a character, put their name in capital letters. This indicates to the judge that they are seeing this person for the first time.

Dialogue has the character's name in capitals around 4.0" from the left margin. The actual dialogue should be indented about 2.7" from the left margin and end 2.4" inches from the right margin. This way, the dialogue should sit in a nice, imaginary box in the middle of the page.

If you need to add any description about their manner of

speaking, as long as it's brief, you can put it under their name in their parenthesis.

```
                    SEAN
                  (stunned)
        I can't believe it, my words are finally
        being    put    into    screenplay    format!
```

If you read other screenplays, and you should be reading produced scripts to hone your skills, you'll see these rules applied. Every writer, no matter how many award-winning scripts they have churned out, has followed these tried and tested rules. It's not about conformity; it's about making the sale of their script easy.

You may be asking yourself, "Why is it so important to follow all this formatting stuff? I just want to write." It may seem like a bunch of silly rules, but they could spell the difference between winning and losing a contest.

There are two main reasons for these formatting rules.

First, if you can't follow some basic rules that are in place for everyone's benefit, then you probably don't know how to write. This may come across as overly harsh, but I've found this to be true. Out of the *thousands* of scripts that I have read, not a single script with significant formatting errors has come close to dazzling me with incredible storytelling or a High Concept premise.

I'm still waiting for that day to happen, but so far, nothing.

Second, once you enter a screenwriting competition, it isn't all about you. It's about making life easy for the contest judge.

Ever visited different doctors' offices and had to fill out their paperwork? They all have different forms. The information they are requesting is usually the same, but the sheets have different columns or some are double-sided. Wouldn't it be great if all doctors used a standard form? Of course, that would make things easier for you.

Reading for a contest can be a very arduous task. This isn't to say that my role as a contest job is drudgery. I enjoy reading a wide variety of material and I'm always looking for that one script that I want to win the contest.

Over the years, I've found that I've been able to read scripts at a much faster rate, provided that they are formatted properly. My eyes are trained to read Courier 12-point font. The reason for it is that each character takes up the exact same amount of space on a page, regardless of what character they are.

For example, a period "." takes up the same real estate as a capital "Z." Other fonts expand and contract the characters depending on whether or not they are capitalized or are simply more slender, such as the letter "I" versus a capital "T."

HERE IS AN EXAMPLE OF THE ARIAL FONT.
here is an example of the arial font.

```
HERE IS AN EXAMPLE OF THE COURIER FONT.
here is an example of the courier font.
```

Do you notice the difference? When the Arial font is in lowercase, the letters get squeezed closer together. Courier is referred to as a mono-spaced font, while Arial is a variable-width font.

Arial can be a little more difficult to read. That may not be a problem if you are reading a couple of pages, say in an email or a short report. However, screenplays are between ninety to one hundred and twenty pages. Multiply that by two hundred or more scripts and the page count quickly adds up.

Maintaining the same spacing makes it easier on the judge's eyes. In this manner, I am able to *absorb* words. This concept is a bit difficult to explain. Words are not sounded out in my head, there isn't a running narrative since I'm not hearing each word. Instead, my eyes are able to look at a block of text and I understand immediately what the writer is saying.

For those of you who are fluent in more than one language, it's the difference between hearing a foreign word and translating it into English, versus having the ability to think in that language. I'm able to think in blocks of text. When you are at a traffic light, you don't say to yourself, "The light is red, so I must remain stopped until it turns green." The color red in that context is a symbol. You know what it means without thinking about it. For me, entire sentences can be absorbed as one symbol, not individual words to be sounded out.

Having the dialogue in the middle portion of the page automatically tells me that people are talking. It's more efficient than quotations. Capital letters on one line tell me that it's a location. Margin to margin text indicates that you are describing something.

Any change in the font or how the screenplay is formatted can throw off the *absorption* process. You may have the best written script out there, but if it's presented poorly you won't have the judge's complete attention.

Sean Hinchey

Many writers think that by changing the formatting, their writing will stand out. Here's the problem: you never want to stand out in a negative way. Let your story telling and concept lead you to success, not clever changes to the formatted words on the page.

All of these issues can be avoided if you use any of the screenwriting formatting software that is currently available. Use the default settings and you won't have any problems. If you are using regular writing software, simply set your tabs, margins, and fonts properly and you're good to go. Realize that screenwriting is a form of technical writing. Proper formatting helps the reader digest the information because it is laid out in a manner that they understand.

If you make it easier for us to read your script, the judges will make it easier for you to win.

SCRIPT PACKAGING

How you package your script can be very important in not only successfully winning a writing contest, but also for getting your script to the right person. Just as formatting exists for a specific reason, so does packaging. For many screenwriting contests, electronic files are becoming more the norm.

If you do submit an electronic version, convert your script to a PDF file, and make sure that all of the formatting is maintained before you send it out. If you write your script in word processing software or proprietary screenwriting software, not everybody may have that program to open your file. PDF is universal.

There are still a significant number of competitions that want a hard copy. These rules apply to submitting your script to a production company, agency, or a specific actor you wish to get attached to your material. So, do it right the first time.

Buy the paper that is already *three hole punched*. As a writer, you probably have reams of paper filling your closets. When it's on sale, you buy even more of it. However, resist the temptation to use your regular paper and punch out the holes yourself.

Why is that? You will be binding the entire screenplay with two, not three, but two brass brads on the top and bottom holes. If you try to punch out the holes yourself—even with a high quality hole punch machine—the holes will not line up.

Most hole punch devices allow you to insert ten or so pages at a time. Each set of paper that is put into the machine gets slightly out of alignment with the last batch of paper that you punched. When you go to bind your screenplay, the pages will look rough around the edges, instead of having a clean, book-like feel to it. To make matters worse, as the pages are turned, they will get bound up.

There is an exception to the rule about using regular paper that isn't pre-punched. Many photocopying shops will use standard paper when photocopying your scripts. They have industrial drills and presses that will create the perfect hole punch allowing your script to have a professional presentation.

Make sure you use brads of sufficient length. Usually, 1.5" brass brads are fine, unless your script is over one hundred and twenty pages. If the brads are too short, the script will fall apart before a judge can read page five.

This has happened to me on too many occasions. I've had to gather up the scattered pages, reorder them, and use my own brads to put the script together. What kind of mood do you think I was in when it came time to judge that screenplay?

You may want to consider printing out your script, and having it photocopied for submission. Many laser and inkjet printers tend to curl the page and make it hard to lay flat so they can be read. If you go this route, they can produce the copies on three hole paper.

Never get fancy with your parchment. While it may be tempting to use something much bolder and of finer quality, you will not only be wasting your time, but it may prevent you from getting what you want. In other words, winning! Paper is very tactile. Any linen type of paper can have an unusual feel to it. Do not use off-white or cream color paper. Black text on standard 92 brightness, white paper has a nice contrast to it, which makes it easy for everyone to read. Heavier weight papers can distract from the reading process as a judge flips through your screenplay. It makes the pages to hard to turn.

All of these points also tie into photocopying. The reason screenplays are put together with brads is so they can be easily taken apart and photocopied, and the original quickly rebound. Heavier paper can jam up a photocopy machine.

Wouldn't it be a shame if someone didn't read your script because it was jamming up the copier for the third time? While most contests won't photocopy your screenplay, do it professionally the first time so it's ready to present to anyone who requests it.

Finally, do use a heavy card stock cover on the front and back of your script. The covers can be punched out by a high quality, consumer hole punch machine. Since it's only two pages, they will line up with the script. Don't try to stand out with your covers. Use a basic white or black cover and don't print any information on the cover. When scripts get photocopied, they may not necessarily get their exact cover back. You don't want to risk that the title of your script gets put on a different script.

Why do all these rules exist about something as simple as how to present your script? Understand how a contest judge reads your screenplay.

Most people hate reading at their desk. I prefer reading on a couch, in bed, or on the floor with a pillow propping up my head. It's easy to cradle the spine of the script with my left hand, while flipping through the pages with the right hand.

If the pages are longer than the standard length, it's difficult to hold. If the pages aren't punched out properly, the script will bind up, as mentioned before. Struggling with pages just to try to get them to turn properly, without them flopping back, is not a fun experience. It's like a CD skipping when you are listening to a song. You are constantly pulled out of the moment.

If your screenplay is the only one out of the thousands of contest scripts that is difficult to read because of a simple packaging issue, do you think that would increase or decrease your chances of advancing to the next round? Keep it clean and basic. Your script will have its chance to be read by the contest judge. I can promise you that.

PAGE COUNT

Screenplays come in all different lengths. There is a sweet zone that should be your target. However, there is an exception that will be discussed later in this chapter.

The minimum length of any script should be around ninety pages. There is an entire section of this book that delves into Screenplay Structure. For now, know that a screenplay is broken up into Three Acts. Act One comprises roughly 25% of your total screenplay. The Second Act is 50% of the script, with 25% going to the final, Third Act of your script.

At ninety pages, that means that the page count for Acts One, Two, and Three are at pages twenty-two, forty-four and twenty-two, respectively. Twenty-two pages is a sufficient amount of time to set up your characters and conflict, and should provide enough space to springboard the story into the Second Act. The proportion of pages left over offers plenty of opportunity to tell the bulk of the story and wrap things up. What happens if you deliver a script that is shorter than ninety pages? An eighty page screenplay doesn't have enough time to thoroughly tell a story.

For the most part, very few screenplays come in too short. However, if you find that you're writing a lot of filler to bring your story up to a certain minimum number of pages, recognize that you may not have enough subject matter to make for an interesting script.

The movie *Julie and Julia (2009)* had two interesting components to it that made the story work. One was the story of Julia Child writing her famous cookbook, and the other was a young woman who cooked every single recipe from that cookbook. Neither story on its own was interesting enough to sustain an entire movie. The two storylines, which were cleverly stitched together, made for a very enjoyable movie. If your script is too short, maybe you need to add another thread to the story.

The majority of scripts come in longer than they should, which can jeopardize your chances of winning a contest. How long should your screenplay be? If you write a one hundred and twenty page script, you are safe in terms of overall length. Going back to the structure breakdown, the First, Second and Third Acts would come in at thirty, sixty, and thirty pages, respectively.

Are contest judges strict about the length of a screenplay? The answer is both yes and no.

Let's talk about the "yes" factor first. Every contest judge flips to the last page of the screenplay to see how long a read they are in for. It's like looking at the prices on a menu before you figure out what you are going to order.

The formatting of a screenplay is roughly one minute of screen time per page of written material. Therefore, a one hundred and twenty minute script is a two-hour movie. That's a nice length, plenty of time to tell a solid story, without going too long.

There's a certain length of time that is the sweet spot for holding a person's attention for entertainment value. This could be for a live concert, sporting event, or a stage play. Too short, and it's over too soon, leaving the audience unfulfilled. Too long, and the audience's attention starts to wane and the impact of the story is diminished.

This brings us to the second answer to the question: Are

contest judges strict about your screenplay's length? Judges don't always care about the length. What they look for is a great read—solid characters, great concept and crisp pacing.

However, if your script comes in at one hundred and forty-three pages, it better be an Academy Award-winning script or the next *Magnolia* (1999). You will find that your script will warrant closer scrutiny because of the higher page count. Why does this hold true?

If you generate one hundred and forty pages, for example, you are telling the judge that your script is so good, so worth the payoff, that you needed more pages to tell your story than anyone else. Your demand for more pages, and thus more time on behalf of the contest judge, has created the expectation of sheer brilliance on your part. You better deliver.

As an example of this, let's look at a restaurant scenario. If you order a hamburger and it takes fifteen minutes for it to arrive, you are probably fine with that. At most restaurants that serve paella, the order can take forty minutes to an hour for it to arrive. A wait that long creates a higher expectation of excellence. If it's prepared wrong, then you feel cheated.

Summer blockbuster movies have tickled the three-hour mark for films. James Cameron's last two films have logged almost six hours of screen time together. Many of the films based around comic book superheroes are well over two hours. Biopic movies run a little long because there is so much to cover when revealing an iconic figure's life. However, these examples have had solid attachments to them that make the page count moot. It could be that the material is based on a best-selling book or has an A-List actor or director attached to the project.

This does not hold true for you. You are offering a screenplay to a script writing contest, not a production company. Right there is the difference. Out of all the contest submissions that have passed before me, I have never read one that was over one hundred and thirty pages that was great. They didn't get dumped into the recycle bin because of their length. I passed on those scripts because they were too verbose. To put this in context, *Schindler's List (1993)* came in at one hundred and twenty-six pages.

Keep in mind that when crafting your next screenplay for an upcoming script contest, see if you nail the sweet spot between ninety to one hundred and twenty pages. If you are over by a few pages, a quick nip and tuck can bring your page count down.

Let your writing stand out, not your page count.

PITCHING

Pitching is an art form that can be learned. Next to having the ability to write a quality script, you need to be able to clearly pitch your screenplay.

There are **Three Solid Reasons** for this, and the arguments of the naysayers against pitching will be discussed as well. Before we begin, realize that pitching is another valuable tool to use in your quest to win a screenwriting contest and ultimately sell your product. It can also help you craft a better screenplay.

It's not necessary to turn yourself into a pitching machine. There are many people who can rattle off pitches all day long as if it's second nature to them. The purpose of learning this art is to help you get what you want.

The first reason for being able to pitch your story is that you are crafting a solid synopsis or logline of your entire screenplay. Before you begin hammering out a draft of the script, you should be working up a solid one-line and three-line pitch of the story.

The one-line pitch is the *TV Guide* synopsis of your story similar to what one would read in either *TV Guide*, IMDB.com, or the description when you select a movie on cable or satellite TV.

They go something like this: "A man will stop at nothing to prove the innocence of his incarcerated wife."

What does this pitch tell you about the movie? It's a drama, for one thing, there's nothing to indicate that it's a spoof or satire. There's some element of true love involved, possibly some action, but it may be more of a detective type of movie along the lines of *The Fugitive (1993)*. If you change "A man" to "A group of mercenaries," then you would have visions of an action movie with high-octane explosions.

This one-line pitch has encapsulated what the movie is about in terms of character development, tone, and plot. The secret to doing this is to keep the pitch simple and focused on *what the main character wants*. More will be discussed about the *want* or *goal* of the main character in a later chapter. For now, let's stick with the art of the pitch.

You can expand on this idea by developing a three-line pitch. The remaining two lines could be something like: "After uncovering evidence of a frame-up he decides to go after the people behind the conspiracy. What he discovers is more sinister and reveals a plot bigger than himself and his wife."

Now the story is even more defined. There's revenge involved, conspiracies, and a larger backstory. The tone of the script is further revealed, and the pitch will either draw the viewer in or leave them looking for something else to read and/or watch. Either way, you've efficiently communicated a great deal of information about your story.

The second reason for being able to pitch your story is, if you can't pitch it, it probably isn't worth writing. Plenty of writers would disagree with this statement, but no producer would.

One reason against relying too much on pitching is that a script may have too many nuances that cannot be summarized in a single, or three-line, pitch. Another argument is that relying on a pitch may cause the other person to prejudge the material based on too little information. Yet another argument says that if a party doesn't have time to read your script, then they aren't worth your time.

These arguments may have their heart in the correct place, but in reality, they are wrong. We'll break them down individually.

If you are writing a story that has so many nuances that it cannot be pitched, then the script is too busy. To borrow from the previous logline, if you are writing a story about a man who wants to bust his innocent wife out of jail, then that is the crux of the story. Focus on that aspect.

If your pitch wanders and tries to cover too much territory, then your writing isn't effective. For example: "It's a story about a man who is trying to get his wife out of jail so he can reunite his family, go on a trip to Asia that he always dreamed of, get his old job back...."

It's impossible for anyone to write a book or script *about* World War II. There are so many different aspects to it, nobody can get their arms around such a vast period in time. Successful projects have focused on one battle or one key person as it relates to the larger picture. *Saving Private Ryan (1998)* focuses on a platoon trying to save another man against the backdrop of an epic war. The films *Patton (1970), Kelly's Heroes (1970),* and *Letters from Iwo Jima (2007)* are focused on a smaller story in the context of a larger event.

How does this tie into winning a screenwriting contest?

Remember, pitching is a tool that you use to promote your

script. Before getting too deep into a screenplay, write the pitch. Hone it to see what works and what doesn't work. When you create a solid logline before you even write the first scene, you are testing the concept out. This will save you time and give you focus.

It's like painting a room in your home. Before you go out and buy gallons of paint, you get some samples and paint a few swatches on the wall of different colors or different shades of the same color. You examine it over a couple of days to see how it captures the sunlight or goes with your existing furniture. If you painted the entire room first and hated the color, you'd have to either live with it or start over again.

Going back to our logline example: After pitching the idea to other people, you may find that it works better to have the husband in jail, while the wife breaks him out. Or maybe both of them are in different jails and their child has to break them out. Pitching helps you discern what is most important in your story.

The third reason for being able to pitch your script is that the contest judge will have to come up with a logline of your material when they submit their best picks. If you can't come up with a concise synopsis, how can you expect them to be able to? If your pitch is five sentences, the judge's synopsis will probably be at least that long.

The argument against pitching—that it will cause another person to prejudge your script without reading it—is actually a positive aspect. If they don't like the genre or plot, then you are saving everyone precious time. If a production company or agency won't read your material because you don't have a good pitch put together, don't hold that against them. A company that makes comedies isn't going to be interested in your thriller, no matter how good your pitch is.

Look at it this way: a friend of yours comes back from the theater and tells you that you have to see that film right away. What is the first question you ask?

What's the movie about?

If your friend says that it's not important, that you just have to go see it right away, then you may be a little skeptical. Is it a genre you like? Does it have an actor you're interested in seeing? Chances are, you won't go see the movie unless you know at least a little something about it.

Pitching isn't rocket science. Approach pitching the way you would tell your favorite joke. Every time you tell a new group of people a funny story or a joke, you change it a little. Maybe you build up the suspense one time or shorten the delivery another time. However, you always hit the same key points: the setup, the characters, and of course the punch line.

Again, pitching will help you refine your story before you even begin writing it. If you are already writing a script or even have one completed, figure out how you would pitch your idea. Keep it lean and on target. Practice by coming up with pitches of your favorite movies, then apply that template to your own material. In no time, you'll be pitching like a pro.

KEY POINTS

- Winning a contest shouldn't be your ultimate goal. Selling your script is.

- You should always be mulling over ideas for a new screenplay.

- It takes time to read a feature screenplay, so be gracious when discussing feedback on your script.

- Formatting and packaging rules are there to make it easy for the others to read your screenplay.

- If 12-point Courier font is good enough for an Academy Award-winning screenwriter, it's good enough for your script.

- Let your writing stand out, not a flashy cover or colored paper.

- Ninety to one hundred and twenty pages is the sweet zone for any screenplay.

- Longer scripts usually have too much description; shorter ones don't have enough story to them.

- If you can't pitch your script, then your story may be too complex or too thin.

- A pitch may not make or break your script, but as a properly used tool it can help you get in the door.

THREE: PRESENTATION AND PRECAUTIONS

TEXT & STYLE

Scripts are designed to be an easy read. In a previous chapter, font type and size, formatting, and other components regarding how words should be put on paper was discussed. There is another formatting element that can damage your chances of winning a screenwriting contest: having too much description.

How you shape your story through the plot, characters, and conflict can only be revealed in two ways—through the use of description and in dialogue. In the next two chapters we will be specifically addressing these two crucial elements of your script. For now, we are going to look at how the words should appear on your page.

First, you should have space between your blocks of text. Never have more than four or five sentences in paragraph. What you are trying to do is free up more **white space**.

White space is the white color from the paper peeking through in between all of the text. While the words themselves have meaning, how they look and are arranged on the page can also help set the mood for the entire screenplay.

For example, if you have ever read a textbook about computer programming from the 1980s, you'll find that they are usually printed in a small font and are densely packed with words. There are few paragraph breaks which makes the entire read a bit intimidating. Never underestimate the power of good, clear presentation of your material.

Sean Hinchey

Many writers focus solely on their writing skills, and crafting a solid screenplay is very important. How you present your product can make or break your opportunity to win a screenwriting contest. Assume that two scripts are equal: both have a solid story, fantastic concept, great dialogue, and nice pacing. That should guarantee a contest win. But the difference between a winner and a forgotten script can come down to your presentation.

I used to go to a dentist who had a small office, but everything was just a little bit disorganized. The magazines in the waiting room were at least a year old, the hygienist would have to leave me in the dental chair while she grabbed something she forgot, and paying my bill took a bit of time because of their antiquated system. However, I never felt as if my dental health was in jeopardy. The doctor was always prompt and professional and he took good care of my teeth.

Several years later, a move forced me to get a new dentist. His office had a flat screen TV in a spacious waiting room. He had current magazines that were cool: cars, electronic gadgets, and the entertainment industry. Since I was a new patient, the doctor met with me before my cleaning and asked if I had any questions for him. While the hygienist was working on my teeth I was able to watch the news on yet another flat screen TV, which allowed me to relax.

Both experiences allowed me to maintain my dental health. Again, the first dentist never gave me any reason to doubt his medical skills. However, my new dentist created a more relaxing atmosphere. It's not that he was trying to be glittery. It was as if he was letting his patients know that most people hate going to the dentist, and he was willing to do something that made the experience a little less stressful.

What does all this have to do with screenwriting?

There have been many scripts that have dense text on the opening page. They are mostly filled with heavy description, all contained in two paragraphs. It's very intimidating to read. It's like going to a cocktail party and you meet someone who won't stop talking. You can't interject a word into the conversation and you lose track of what they are saying because it's overbearing.

The same goes for words on a page. Instead of creating dense blocks of text, open it up. Have more paragraph breaks and interject your description with dialogue. Going back to the example of the computer book: If you open a newer technology book you'll find that they are more user-friendly. Often times they use diagrams, pictures, or drawings. Many of the books use different font sizes and boldface to highlight different sections. It's easier to absorb the information because the presentation is better. White space allows the script to breathe. A contest judge would rather read a one hundred and twenty-page script that is properly formatted, than a ninety-page screenplay of dense material. There's an old joke about a man who goes to a pizza parlor and orders a large pie with everything on it. The owner asks him, "Would you like that cut into eight slices or twelve?" The man responds, "Oh, I couldn't possibly eat twelve slices."

When it comes to writing good description, stay away from flowery prose. Film is a visual medium, but that doesn't mean you have to get too verbose with your descriptions.

This example is from an actual script: "As she ran across

the field in her favorite dress, she left footprints in the dew on the grass. She collapsed to the ground giggling, staring at the clouds as they traced a path across the impossibly blue sky."

In a novel, such description would be welcomed. The writer is creating a world where readers can not only immerse themselves in the world that is created, but hear a character's thoughts and understand their deepest desires. Such verbose description doesn't work in a screenplay because it slows down the reading process. Just let us know that a girl in a sundress is running across a sunny field.

Why can you get away with such a brief description? Contest judges, managers, and agents have all read hundreds, if not thousands, of screenplays. Their minds are already filled with images; what they need from you is a few keywords to trigger the scene.

Never expend precious space on a page when you can reveal the backdrop in as few words as possible. Trust that the person reading the script will be able to visualize the tapestry that you are creating. On dozens of occasions I've had writers tell me that it's important that they meticulously flesh out a scene because it must come across in a very specific way.

That means that the writer actually wants to direct the movie, which is a whole different mindset than trying to win a screenwriting contest. Impress the judges with brevity. Concise is nice.

DESCRIPTION

We are going to dig deeper into what you should be putting on the page. Throughout the rest of this book, you need to keep in mind that you don't have any space to waste when it comes to telling your story. If you stick to the one hundred and twenty page rule, you have a limited amount of lines to use for description, dialogue, and open white space. Make every word count.

By now, it's no secret that you should only write what can be on the screen. The big secret is that most writers ignore this simple guideline because they are trying very hard to get their point across. We're going to discuss **Two Aspects** about writing only what you can show in the description.

The First Aspect concerns describing a new character. It's not uncommon for a writer to interject information such as "The two men have been best friends since high school" or "After graduating at the top of her class, she was excited about starting her new job" or "He was upset that he had to pay so much for his auto repairs since his credit cards were maxed out and he just lost his job."

These are all real life examples from actual screenplays that have been submitted to high-profile contests. The problem here lies in **telling** the reader something that should be **shown**.

What is the difference between telling someone and showing us something? It's all in the phrasing. Let's look back at the previous examples.

We'll assume that it's very important to the story that a woman graduated at the top of her class. You want the contest judge to understand that she is a very driven person, which is why she will succeed at all costs. If you **tell** the reader this in the description, you won't win the screenwriting contest.

Telling shows that you were lazy early on in the story. If you aren't going to take the time to craft a quality script, why should a judge tune into your story? The job of the writer is to engage the person reading your screenplay. Throwing a piece of information out there, without properly integrating it into the story, does not invite the reader into the world you are creating.

So how do you invite them in? **Show** us that this woman is a successful person. Have a friend or relative look through her yearbook where we see a photo of the woman as class valedictorian. Maybe the woman still has some awards in a room at her home. On the other hand, if you show trophies and ribbons stashed away in a dusty box, it may suggest that she's hiding something about her past.

Nobody likes to have everything laid out for them, and judges enjoy a little detective work. This doesn't mean you have to be cryptic or complex like William Faulkner. However, layering in some details allows us to peel back the layers little by little. It makes your script a journey of discovery.

In the example of the man who has maxed out his credit cards on an auto repair, there are ways to show us and not tell us this information. Why not have the mechanic run the man's credit card, then show it getting declined? The man then hands over another credit card: same thing. If you want to show that the man lost his job, maybe in the back seat of the car is a box with his effects from work: old files, a coffee mug, and a few pictures.

If you are serious about winning a screenwriting contest, you have to show the judges that you have an imagination not only about creating characters, but revealing them to the reader. Even in a novel, the author shows us information in this manner, rather than simply telling us. Granted, they have more space to do this and can be more verbose. Again, it's about allowing the reader to discover the character through these clues.

The Second Aspect about writing this type of narrative concerns showing only what is relevant.

One script that stands out in my mind had descriptions so dense regarding the main character that it read more like a dossier than a screenplay. More importantly, the information put on the page had very little to do with how the characters interacted in the story.

Such description is only relevant if it comes into play later. If a girl grew up without her father, it makes sense if she meets up with him later on, or it somehow impacts her relationships with other men, for example. Therefore, not only is it important **not** to tell us about something in a character's past, don't show it if it doesn't tie into the bigger story.

Another example from a screenplay submission had the main character checking into a hotel. For three pages, we saw a man exit a taxi, enter a hotel, and go to the registration desk. The man gave the receptionist a credit card, received two room keys and instructions on where the elevators were. The man entered the elevator, then walked into his room. Remember, three pages equals three minutes of screen time.

At this point, you should be asking yourself, "What was the point of all that?" In terms of the whole story, there was no point to that sequence of scenes. As I was reading them, I was expecting something dramatic to happen. Perhaps he was going to run into somebody in the lobby. Or, as he tried to check in he would be told, "It looks as though you've already checked in." I was expecting that something *relevant* to the story would happen.

It's not enough to have events simply *happen* in your script. Everything needs to be tied into what the story is about. The previous example did nothing to propel the plot forward. Conversely, it hindered the story because I actually wondered if I missed out on some important detail. Did I not read it correctly? Was there a subtle hint that I glossed over?

In *Michael Clayton (2007)* we see a lawyer who has been trying to silence the protagonist and his friend, preparing for an important meeting. On the bed, she is laying out all of her clothes right down to her underwear. In another scene, we see her rehearsing a speech while putting on makeup.

These scenes aren't thrown in to fill space. We are a voyeur during her private moments. We understand that she is methodical and calculating. Because we witness her attention to detail in different ways, we understand that her preparations aren't a one-time fluke. This is how she operates and functions. If she frets over her business clothes, think of how meticulous she is when it comes to huge corporate decisions.

Let's pretend that we are reading the screenplay. In one version it reads, "She is a high-powered lawyer who leaves nothing to chance. Her desire to rise through the ranks knows no limits. Being a perfectionist she even selects her clothes with great attention to finest detail."

In another version is reads, "Carefully laid out on the bed in front of her is an expensive dress. She absentmindedly chews on her thumbnail, then smoothes out a wrinkle in a silk slip. After laying out a new pair of nylons, she nods to herself, finally satisfied." And in a later scene, "While seated in front of a mirror in her enormous, yet sterile bathroom she practices her speech while applying makeup. Each time she changes the inflection of her voice."

Which version would be more satisfying to you? The second set of descriptions should involve you in the story. Rather than being told what to think, you are able to draw your own conclusions.

In an earlier chapter we discussed the importance of white space on a page. Many writers fill the page with a lot of description. We are talking dense paragraphs, nothing but black letters muddling up the white page. One way to lessen this mass of words is to pull back the description. Keep it lean: It's not necessary to go into great detail on every aspect of your script.

Unless there is an important detail about a building in a scene, it's enough to describe a house as a "quaint home" or an office building as "nondescript." In most cases, the writers expend precious space describing the flower beds around the home, the freshly painted shutters or the spotless driveway. Unless these descriptions have some relevance to other aspects of the screenplay, then simply saying an "immaculate yard" is enough. It's enough description for a contest judge to fill in the blanks.

Sean Hinchey

Another way of creating more white space is by breaking up the paragraphs of text. Generally, if you are going to have more than five lines of text in one paragraph, you are jamming up the page. By simply leaving a blank line in between the paragraphs, you are allowing the script and the reader to "breathe." It gives the contest judge's eyes a break.

Crafting solid description that is relevant to the story is very important because it visually takes up a large portion of the page. When a contest judge flips through a screenplay and sees huge sections of description with no breaks, it makes them dread reading your material. A few simple tweaks can make it inviting to the eyes.

DIALOGUE

Dialogue is more than just having people talk. They are exchanging ideas, their feelings, their goals, and sometimes they even lie. For many writers, putting dialogue down on paper is simply about having people exchange snappy retorts. I used to refer to this as the "*Pulp Fiction* Plague," but more recently it has been updated to "*Juno* Jargon."

I arrived at these terms based on two films, *Pulp Fiction* (1994) and *Juno* (2007) that both contained catchy dialogue. From that point onward, amateur writers began cranking out dialogue with a similar cadence and banter. What they failed to realize is that in both movies, the dialogue went beyond sounding cool; it moved the story forward. It's like jazz musicians who improvise: They actually know a great deal about music.

The secret to writing dialogue is to recognize that conversations between characters are about *action*. We will then approach the art of dialogue from this viewpoint.

Contest judges love great dialogue, the kind of exchanges where people may leave sentences hanging or the characters stammer. They don't always use grammatically-correct English, and they very rarely say what is on their mind. The words should leap off the page, the exchanges quick and crisp. Truly great dialogue drives the story forward like no other aspect of the screenplay. It is the most overlooked and misunderstood part of generating a quality product. Every script that I have pushed forward in the culling process has had excellent dialogue.

How is dialogue a form of action? Remember, in a screenplay there are only two ways for you to tell the story: description and dialogue. People talking to each other is a form of action, because of what they are saying, or perhaps *aren't saying* moves the story forward.

There are **Three Secrets** to writing solid dialogue.

First, the most effective dialogue uses subtext. There are ways to say things without actually saying them. For example, there's a man eating breakfast in a small restaurant. A waiter comes by and begins topping off the coffee. The customer angrily snaps at the waiter, then starts complaining about the eggs being undercooked and the bacon is too crisp. To an outside viewer, we would think that this is a very difficult man to deal with.

However, if you have an earlier scene where we see that the man just lost a major client, or was kicked out of his house, then we see these exchanges in a different light. What appeared to be a man simply flipping out for no reason now has meaning. We understand his plight and his problems. He's not pissed about his breakfast, but about everything *except* breakfast. **Subtext** is about finding a way to say something without actually saying it.

Think about your own life. When was the last time you had an argument with a spouse, significant other, or friend? It could've ignited over something small: the laundry wasn't folded, or the other person was five minutes late meeting you for lunch. You weren't really upset about that specific incident. It was just the straw that broke the camel's back. There was a buildup, then a seemingly small and insignificant episode unleashed someone's wrath.

Procedural shows such as *Law and Order* have incredible amounts of subtext in them. In court scenes, there is often a face-off between one of the lawyers and a defendant on the witness stand. The lawyer may be attacking the credibility of the witness, while the witness strikes back with evasive answers or only answers the questions without elaborating. The lawyer may say, "Earlier, you claimed that you weren't at the crime scene, but now you say you were, but you didn't see anything. So tell us, which part is the truth?" The lawyer can't come out and call the person a liar; it's better to break them down with facts.

The witness, when asked a direct question, may respond with, "You know, I don't remember. It was so dark outside." The audience clearly knows that's not true, but the witness is playing dumb, maybe because they are being forced to testify, or they are afraid of the defendant, or they have something to hide.

In each scene, figure out what you want to accomplish with all the characters who are present. Write down exactly what you want them to say, then find another way of saying it. This isn't about trying to generate snappy, clever dialogue. It's about constructing smart, interesting exchanges.

This is particularly effective in comedy. The legendary writer-director Billy Wilder used to say that people should be talking about any and everything, except what they are talking about. In the film *When Harry Met Sally* (1989), Harry explodes at his two friends, telling them that they shouldn't get married. He goes on to say that at some point in their lives, they'll hate each other and they'll be going to a lawyer to argue over a stupid, wagon wheel coffee table.

It's clear to the audience that he's upset after running

into his ex-wife, who seems to be even happier without Harry. Marie and Jess, the couple being chastised, look on aghast as Harry storms out. Marie looks deeply into Jess's eyes and tells him, "I want you to know I will never want that wagon wheel coffee table."

That one line works for so many reasons. It lightens up a tense moment in the movie. Harry is yelling at his friends over something very serious to them: marriage. But most important, when Marie starts saying, "I want you to know..." one would expect her to say something comforting about how they will never break up, they're in this relationship for the long haul, etc. While it appears that she is directly addressing the coffee table, it's clear to all of us that she is really telling Jess that she loves him.

Using subtext allows the writer to create dialogue that is just a little bit off-center from what the real subject matter is. A good way to understand this further is to just kick back and listen to groups of people when they talk. Often times they'll guard their true intentions or use different words to soften the blow when they speak. People might use sarcasm and then mask it with "I was just kidding," if another person gets offended. People often provoke others or give false praise to come across as sincere when they have negative feelings toward a person. Passive-aggressive dialogue is a form of subtext.

The second secret to creating solid dialogue is to slowly reveal your character through exchanges as the story progresses. A good way of understanding this is by learning what *not* to do. Never give away an entire backstory in any scene. This example is paraphrased from dozens of scripts that I have read. None of them made it past the first round.

A person will say, "Hey, if it isn't my old college roommate, Gail. I haven't seen you in almost ten years. You look the same now as you did while Gary was dating you. What a lucky guy he is now that he married you when he had the chance. I was just thinking about some of the crazy things we did back in those days, it's a wonder we never got put in jail."

This example is not an exaggeration. While the words have been modified slightly to protect the innocent, this example is almost commonplace. In their haste to get all the pertinent information out about the main characters, the writer has explained the entire background as if it were a punch list. Screenplays should never read like bullet points.

A better way of getting this information across is by layering different details into your story. Revealing a character through dialogue is a lot like getting to know someone that you just met. If you were to ask that person a few questions about themselves, and they rambled on for half an hour without even taking a breath, you might find that a little off-putting.

You would rather learn a little bit about them here and there. If they like to travel, then you may spend most of your first conversation with them talking about different countries that both of you may have visited. As time goes on, you'll learn more about them, and they will understand who you are.

I read an article recently about a group of people who were working together at a research base in Antarctica. The rule was that nobody could talk about themselves for more than fifteen minutes per day. The reason was that they would all be isolated with only one another for the next six months. If everyone knew too much about the other people, there would be nothing left to learn, which would lead to boredom. By limiting the amount of information exchanged, they could lengthen that journey of discovery.

In a script, you don't have that much time to fully understand who the characters are. It isn't going to take six months to read. It better not. There isn't a hard and fast formula about how you reveal a character through dialogue. The best way to go about this is by examining some of your own relationships.

How did you first meet your best friend? In the early months you probably kept everything fun and light. As time progressed you were able to talk to them about serious stuff, such as a bad breakup or problems at home. After even more time, they were the person you went to when you had no one else to turn to.

Don't be afraid to draw on your life experiences. That's what makes a script genuine and adds depth to your story and characters. The best dialogue sounds real, as if the reader is eavesdropping on something that wasn't meant for their ears.

The third secret to writing solid dialogue is by having your character say one thing, when they really should be saying something else. The unsaid becomes the proverbial elephant in the room.

For example, if a child got suspended from school and he is sitting at the dinner table, it would be expected that his suspension would be the topic of conversation. If the parents gloss over the issue and talk about other unimportant events, that speaks volumes about the family dynamic. They could be avoiding it because they don't know how to handle their son, or they could be afraid of him. Whatever the reason is, having characters *not* talk about something so obvious can say more than if someone actually says it.

This is used in films where there is a specific hierarchy among the characters. The leader of the group may make an obvious mistake or act in a questionable manner. However, nobody points this out. This speaks so much about the power of this leader—nobody will challenge this person. This mechanism was used a great deal in *Casino (1995)*. There is so much that the casino owner could and should be saying to his smart-mouthed enforcer. The reason he doesn't is partly out of fear, partly out of loyalty.

At some point, everything will be laid on the line, in a very on-the-nose manner. For example, in *Planes, Trains & Automobiles (1987)*, we learn at the end of the movie that the supporting character's wife died years ago, and he's a loner who just travels around the country. This is handled very well because this man is coming clean with the protagonist after all their adventures together. Toward the end of the story, a character can speak plainly. It's usually part of a big payoff, the moment of truth so there's no need to craft off-center dialogue.

Before you decide that your script is ready to be submitted, read the dialogue aloud. Sometimes words sound different in your head than they do when they are spoken. You may encounter a tongue twister, or the cadence may seem weird. Actually speaking the words helps you to put that final polish on your dialogue. If you stumble over some lines, rewrite them.

Sean Hinchey

Now that you are aware of the secrets, next time you watch a movie you will see how they are brought into play. The more realistic you can make your dialogue, the more it will ring true for the contest judges. Make them want you to win.

WATCH YOUR TONE

When you first begin writing your screenplay, it should be easy to figure out what the genre is. It's not often that you start typing and decide you're going to switch from a period piece to a contemporary comedy. The subject matter often dictates what genre your script will fall under.

However, a key element that is missing from many contest-submitted scripts is that the proper **tone** of the story isn't maintained. Tone may be one of those words you've heard thrown around before, but it may not always be used properly.

At some point in our lives we've all been chastised by someone who didn't like the tone of our voice. Perhaps we had an edge of sarcasm to it, were a bit shrill, exasperated or short. Many people confuse the tone of their story as having to do with dialogue. That's not what we'll be discussing here.

Tone has to do with the **mood** of the story. You need to set the tone very early on and you cannot change it. If it does change, it can be very jarring for the contest judge, and as a result it will pull them out of the world you've created.

Here's an example of tone. Suppose you receive an invitation to a formal cocktail party written in calligraphy on expensive parchment. In preparation for the evening, you break out your best clothes, or maybe even buy something new just for that party. You make sure you are all put together for a wonderful evening. Once inside the party, there's a string quartet playing music while waiters and waitresses wearing white gloves are serving drinks.

Sean Hinchey

The entire mood of the party is exactly what you would've expected. Nobody is dressed in jeans, and people are sipping fancy drinks from crystal clear glasses without a keg in sight. Finger foods are brought around to each guest. The conversation in the room has a low murmur to it. If this were a movie, then we would've established the tone of the entire event.

The host of the party asks the audience for their attention as the quartet stops playing. After thanking everyone for attending the party, he or she announces that there is a wonderful surprise in store. On cue, a group of clowns flow into the room. They honk their noses, make animals out of balloons, and cause a fair amount of harmless mischief. Meanwhile, the waiters are now offering cotton candy, fried Twinkies and caramel apples to the guests.

This would make for a memorable party, but probably not in a good way. Having clowns show up at a formal cocktail party would ruin the entire mood of the event. It's not the tone you were expecting. Instead of having a fancy night out, a carnival atmosphere has popped up. You'd probably find that the party would clear out rather quickly. Besides, who wants to get caramel on a tuxedo?

There would be an expectation that certain events would unfold throughout the evening. Clowns were not one of those expectations. This doesn't mean you can't have surprises at a cocktail party or in your script. What if the host had said that there was a big surprise in store for the guests, then asked each person to look under the chair that they were sitting on? Taped under each chair at each table was a gift card for a nice restaurant in town. Or, only one chair had a card under it that allowed that person to take home the centerpiece. Those surprises would be in relation to the mood or tone of the entire evening.

There was a movie trailer for the film *Kick Ass (2010)*, which was about a high school student who decided he wanted to be a superhero in real life. The trailer made it seem as if the film was going to be a satire on the entire superhero movie genre. While it did have its funny moments, I found most of the movie to be very dark. There are some gruesome scenes where people are killed, and one of the superheroes has a very bleak home life.

None of this is the fault of the screenwriters. This has to do with how the marketing team presented this movie in the advertisements. The same issue came up with *Return to Me (2000)*, which was marketed as a comedy, but was mostly a very heavy film. The tone was different from what was expected.

As a writer, you have to keep whatever tone you've established early in the story consistent all the way through to the end. How can you gauge that you are doing this successfully?

You need to make sure you've properly established the *suspension of disbelief*. Many scripts take place in a contemporary setting, one based on reality as we know it. Other scripts contain events that defy the laws of physics or even common sense. In an action movie, you will have car chases, gunplay, and hand-to-hand fighting. When setting up the tone of these stories, you need to firmly plant the reality of this world by constructing the proper suspension of disbelief.

Raiders of the Lost Ark (1981) begins with an archaeologist trying to find an ancient treasure. In the opening sequence we see darts fly from walls, gigantic spiders, and a huge bolder that chases him out of the cavern. Immediately, we are aware that this will be a fun, rollercoaster ride of a movie. We accept the fact that most anything can happen. However, the tone is set up in such a manner that if a huge spaceship were to appear shooting lasers, that would be out of place in this story. We are talking about the original film, not *Indiana Jones and the Kingdom of the Crystal Skull (2008)*, which has a significantly different tone.

In comedy, the series *Sex in the City* is about a group of women friends living in New York sharing secrets. The stories revolve around love, dating, and work. At least, this is what I've been told. In this setting, we very rarely see any of them actually working, unless it relates directly to the story. They all have fabulous lives that involve shopping, drinking, and exchanging gossip.

As written, these women have an enormous amount of free time on their hands. But this world is a fantasy. It's fun for people to lose themselves in this make-believe creation. The amount of money these women spend on their cocktails alone is greater than the income of most tycoons. How the writer sets up this background allows for anything to happen regarding the life of luxury and self-indulgence. If one of the girls suddenly stopped hanging out with the others because their co-op was in foreclosure and their credit cards were maxed out, it wouldn't work in this setting. Again, it's a fantasy show, not a *Real Housewives* franchise, or so I've been told.

Going back to the cocktail party example: If you were to establish that the host of the lavish get-together was an eccentric prankster, then having the black-tie affair turn into a circus would be acceptable. It could work in *54 (1998)*, but not in *Mommie Dearest (1981)*.

As you re-read your material, look for any loose fragments that suddenly jar your script out of the reality that you've created. One common example that I often see is a sudden time shift. For example, a slice of life script that I read had a group of friends struggling with car payments, mortgages, and raising kids. It started out with a good setup, but by the middle of the second act, we are thrust five years into the future. There are several other jumps that happen, so that by the end of the story, we are twenty years ahead from where we started.

The writer moved too far forward in the story, too late in the storytelling process. Had the first act been crafted to reflect these time shifts, the reader would've been better prepared for the gigantic leaps. It's all about setting the right foundation. The writer had one character trying to get their child to do well in junior high. When the shift happens, we learn that the child, now an adult, is doing fairly well in college. When a writer plants small details like that in a story, it leads the reader to believe that we will be seeing something very significant about the time we've now landed in.

A time shift based around this type of situation would work if a person is graduating, then being dropped off at college, suitcase in hand and a few dollars in the pocket, all in one concise sequence. We then see them starting their first day of a new job and the story continues on from there. Then, the story unfolds almost like a montage.

Establishing and maintaining the tone of your script makes your story easy to read. When the tone falters throughout the script, it becomes apparent to a contest judge that something is amiss. Tone is an often overlooked element to screenwriting because most writers aren't aware of the impact it can have on their material.

Sean Hinchey

Tone is the boundary of the world you've created. You can push the lines out as far as you want, but make sure you color within them. Maintain the tone and you will have a fantastic baseline to build your story upon.

VOICE-OVER

As I've said before, screenplays only have a limited amount of time and space to tell their story. There's a great deal of exposition that has to be formed by the writer: character development, plot, goal of the protagonist, and so on. There is a temptation to complete some of the groundwork by using **Voice-over**. It may only happen once, or it could come up throughout the screenplay. I would caution any writer attempting to use this device.

Using voice-over is very hard to do well. There needs to be a certain cadence to the dialogue and it needs to be the type of story that lends itself to the use of this mechanism.

One example of it being used well is when the movie is a reflection and we are hearing the protagonist speak as if they are reading from a journal. Voice-over was used properly in *Dances with Wolves (1990)* and *The Last Samurai (2003)*. Because both movies revolved around a time that most people aren't familiar with, the audience required a great deal of information to set up the story. Although there were many visual cues, the voice-over helped set the tone of the story.

In *Dances with Wolves*, the main character is alone for the first act of the movie. Who would he be talking to and why? Hearing him speak about his time on the frontier was soothing, and it helped lay the foundation for the rest of the story. It also presented a very slow unfolding of his character.

The danger with using voice-over is that the words are very on-the-nose. In an earlier chapter regarding dialogue, we discussed the pitfalls of using words spoken by a character that reveal exactly what is going on. Voice-over doesn't use subtext.

Another reason for staying away from voice-over is that it is usually written to cover up for sloppy writing elsewhere in the script. Writing good, believable voice-over is not an easy task. It has to be more than just a running monologue about what the protagonist is thinking or feeling. It's imperative that there is absolutely no other way the reader can gather the information contained in the voice-over.

All of the voice-over laden scripts that I've read have contained information that is redundant. In other words, the reader is already aware of the material contained in the voice-over through other mechanisms. In *Adaptation* (2002), screenplay writing teacher Robert McKee says, "God help you if you use voice-over in your work, my friends. That's flaccid, sloppy writing." I may not go quite that far, but consider yourself cautioned.

Many times, the voice-over tries to be ironic or witty. Never use voice-over simply to illustrate how clever you are as a writer. Never.

Voice-over can slow the storytelling process instead of enhancing it. This is because the information isn't relevant to the story. Voice-over shouldn't be used as a "cool factor"; it must propel the plot forward.

For example, one script that I judged used voice-over in the opening scene. The writer attempted to set up the story by giving a background that never came into play. We learned about the protagonist's childhood, her estrangement from her father, and her current job as a young, single woman in a medium sized city. There were major problems with this setup.

The information that was revealed through the voice-over mechanism would've worked better in another way. For her to **tell** us about these events in her life wasn't as effective as showing us. Other people at work could've talked about visiting parents for the holidays and she may have remained silent during this conversation. Eventually, this sticking point in her family dynamic would've been revealed.

Regarding her job, the opening sequence shows her going to work. If the writer had crafted the office scenes differently, we could've seen how the character responded to her work environment. In one brief scene we would understand whether she likes her job or hates it. An easy way for us to understand her current relationship status would've been a throwaway line about another date gone bad, or she could've deleted an email about speed-dating, swearing that off for the time being.

The biggest problem with that voice-over opening of the story is that none of the issues, except for her romantic life, came into play for the rest of the script. With a setup where she is talking about her estranged father, one would think that would be a large part of her journey through the script. It's never addressed again; there's no awkward phone call from him trying to set things right. It never appears to have scarred her when it comes to dating. Wouldn't there be relationship issues she'd have to contend with? The voice-over served no purpose to the script. Had it been removed entirely, the story wouldn't have suffered. Its presence wasn't relevant to the flow, and in fact, many times it detracted from the storytelling process.

Sean Hinchey

This isn't to say that voice-over should never be used. Certain types of movies call for a voice-over sequence. Earlier, we talked about their use in historic pieces, as in the reading of a journal entry. Voice-overs can add that "gumshoe, private eye" tone to detective stories. The classic film noir genre, such as the Humphrey Bogart movies, illustrates the effectiveness of voice-over when it's embedded into the very fabric of the storytelling. In a sense, it bridged the gap between the visual story telling of film and the descriptive license of literature.

This isn't to suggest that all detective films need to have voice-over. *Chinatown (1974)* and *LA Confidential (1997)* successfully tell their stories without the use of this technique. *Blade Runner (1982)*, a detective film set in a dystopian future, had voice-over throughout the entire story in the original theatrical release. While *Blade Runner* has had seven different versions over the years, with Ridley Scott's "Final Cut" in 2007 being the last, one version had removed the voice-over completely. The movie worked just as well without this device.

Voice-over can be an effective tool in structuring the narrative. Many writers assume that this is an easy device to utilize. This is contrary to reality. Crafting relevant, concise and effective voice-over is a difficult task. It is often overused, or simply poorly executed.

The whole point of adding voice-over is to elevate the storytelling in your screenplay, not eliminate your script from the contest. Before embarking on any voice-over in your screenplay, ask yourself two questions. First, is there any other way you can get across the information in the voice-over through different means? If the answer is yes, no matter how difficult it may be, then utilize those other ways. And second, does the voice-over enhance

Write It to Win It!

your story telling? Never use voice-over simply to make your screenplay look cool or because you feel that the genre you are writing requires it. Contest judges are looking for all around solid writing, free from gimmicks. Let your story idea and execution do the talking, not poorly written voice-over.

One final note regarding the use of voice-over. Certain films employ the mechanism of the *unreliable narrator*. This is when the person narrating may not be telling the audience the truth. The purpose in doing this is to lead the viewer down one path, then create a dramatic twist at the end. A great example of this is *Rashomon (1950)*, where we see an event told through the eyes of all the people present. In the end, the audience still doesn't know what the truth is. *Citizen Kane (1941)* has different witnesses to the protagonist's complex life tell their view of what happened. But what is true and what is embellished? *Usual Suspects (1995)*, *Fight Club (1999)*, and *American Psycho (2000)* all utilize the unreliable narrator.

Again, the main purpose is to lead the audience astray so that the writer can unleash that "Gotcha!" moment. In these types of stories, it's as if that dramatic moment was developed, then worked backwards to craft a story around it. Like a magician working on a trick, the key is to draw the audience's attention elsewhere so that they won't tune in to the secret, the magical payoff. However, just like a good magic show, the audience needs to be dazzled by the pageantry. A good magician puts on an excellent show; they don't just go through the paces to reach the climax of their act. They work the audience into a froth until they can't wait to have their mind blown.

Unfortunately for most writers, the use of the unreliable narrator is the only part that their script has going for it.

Sean Hinchey

If you decide to use this device, your story has to have all of the other elements working in its favor to make the payoff come to fruition. Otherwise, the audience will have left the building long before the big reveal.

FLASHBACKS

In screenwriting contests, the flashback is another overused and poorly-executed storytelling device. If you didn't like what I had to say about voice-overs, then you are going to hate this chapter.

When used effectively, flashbacks can propel the storytelling process forward and add to the richness of your script. Like any other aspect of writing done wrong, a poorly executed flashback can drag your screenplay down to the bottom of the recycling bin.

Flashbacks need to create tension as they transport the reader back in time before snapping us forward to the present. Perhaps we don't learn everything we need to know in a single flashback, and it leaves the reader wanting more. You can use it again in your story.

But before you decide to us it, ask yourself if its use is relevant to your storytelling. For example, I once read a script that used flashbacks extensively throughout the story. We learned about the plight of a young man who was starting out in the working world. In one scene, we learn that he is afraid to let anybody know who he is because he was picked on in high school. We then go into a flashback where the boy is beat up after school. When he gets home his father is indifferent to the boy's run-in at school. The problem with this flashback is that we didn't learn anything new about this father-son dynamic.

In the next scene, written in the present, we know enough about the indifference of his father when it comes to the two of them discussing the death of the young man's mother. What could've made the flashback work is if we had witnessed a different piece of unknown information that tied into the rest of the story.

What if, in the present, the son is trying to be a musician and we see him with a beat up guitar that he bought second hand? In the flashback we see the father indifferent to his son having his first guitar destroyed by the bullies. Maybe the father even goes so far as to refuse his son's pleas to borrow money to buy another used guitar. In the present scene, we would understand how much this musical instrument means to the young man. It shows the protagonist's perseverance set against his traumatic upbringing. This is an example of making a flashback relevant to the rest of the screenplay.

When asking yourself if the flashback is relevant to your story, delve into your material to understand how it will increase the work flow of your entire script. Again, flashbacks shouldn't be used for the "wow" factor. Judges are only impressed by great storytelling.

Is there another way to tell the story, other than using flashbacks? Even if you answer yes to this question, it isn't necessarily a deal breaker. *Citizen Kane (1941)* could have been written in a chronological fashion. All the information would've been revealed, just in a different way. However, the impact of that story would have been dramatically different. The story starts with "Rosebud" and ends with "Rosebud." It revolves around a journalist trying to figure out the true measure of an enigmatic man.

If your story can be told chronologically but there is a better way to establish tension by using the flashback, then make it work for you. Be sure that you stay on course. Make the flashbacks relevant to the core of what your story is about.

How does the use of the flashback enhance the art of storytelling? In *Citizen Kane* we find out what Rosebud is by the end, but it's the journey of traveling through Kane's life that makes the story interesting. For all his wealth, influence, and power, we figure out that what he missed most was his sled. However, it wasn't the sled as a physical entity that he missed, but the simplicity of a childhood he didn't have and a mother's love that he missed out on.

Have the impact of using flashbacks in your script build up to a big reveal. Judges like a good payoff, something with a twist. Think along the lines of *Memento* (2000) or *The Sixth Sense* (1999).

Flashbacks should only be used to expose something that we don't previously know. For example, if there is a scene where a character is talking about something that happened to him in the past, we shouldn't see a flashback that reinforces this point. Instead, think about having a character talk about one thing happening, but in the flashback we see something different. This was used well in a television drama, *Boomtown*, where a woman, who had been on the run for decades, was caught by the police. She was involved in a bank robbery organized by a radical group in which a police officer was shot and killed point blank. The woman, now a devoted mother and active in her community, admits her involvement but denies killing anyone when she was young.

Through a series of flashbacks from different viewpoints we see what happened on that fateful day. The woman accepts a guilty plea but begs her family to accept her version of the story, that she never killed anyone. The final scene is a flashback that shows her with a smoking shotgun as the police officer falls to the ground.

Every flashback scene in that episode presents new and exciting information. We never see the woman talking about her questionable past; instead, we see it happen upon reflection and it saves the final twist until the very last scene.

Surprisingly, many scripts have a flashback within the first few pages. If a flashback is going to be used so early in the screenplay, then why not simply start the story in the past and tell it chronologically? This is a clear example of using this device as a gimmick. Flashbacks require smart writing, not clever usage to try to dazzle the contest judge.

Before utilizing flashbacks, watch as many movies as you can that employ it. Understand why the writer chose that mechanism, looking beyond the "wow factor." A solid understanding of how to use flashbacks sparingly can make your script stand out and may propel your screenplay to the top of the pile. A poorly executed flashback sequence can damage your chance to make it to winner's circle. Do it right, or don't even attempt it.

KEY POINTS

- Ample white space allows the reader room to breathe.

- Don't get overly descriptive; the person reading your script will understand what you are saying.

- Florid prose is great for novels, bad for scripts. And, if it's not relevant to the story, then don't write it.

- Don't try to dazzle the judge with snappy retorts that don't move the story forward.

- Subtext is about saying one thing when you mean something else.

- Maintain the tone of your story from beginning to end in alignment with the genre of your script.

- Suspension of disbelief only works if you establish this from the very first page.

- Voice-over should only be used if it enhances the story, not for the "cool" factor. Remember, if the information can be illustrated through a device other than voice-over, then skip the VO.

- Flashbacks should only reveal information that we won't see elsewhere in the screenplay. Flashbacks are best used to lead the audience one way, only to reveal the truth later on: the twist.

FOUR: STRUCTURE

THE WANT

What is the **want** in a script? Very simply, it is the goal of the main character, it's what they want. I've asked many writers, what does your protagonist want? Obviously, the answers vary based on their story. However, the responses are generally along the lines of "He wants to reunite with his old girlfriend and go off to military so he can make something of himself in the hopes that he can deal with the tragic death of his grandfather who always wanted his grandson to make his mark on the world."

Right away, can you see what is wrong with this goal? There are **Four Problems** that most writers create for themselves when crafting a want for their protagonist. Stay away from these issues, and you'll be well on your way to creating a great script.

First, the want has to be something tangible. In this example there is one element that may work for that particular script. A person wanting to reunite with an old flame is something real. You can put your finger on it. This is what is meant by tangible. It doesn't have to be something physical, like a car or a pile of money. Rather, it has to be something that can actually be understood or realized by the reader of your material.

The other aspect of this want-dealing with the death of his grandfather-will not work for this script or for any other. Very often, it is the type of emotional goal that attempts to drive the story forward in submitted scripts that never make it past the first round. Why doesn't it work?

They key word here is "emotional." It's hard to engage

the reader by having the protagonist try to deal with a hardship. The only way to do this is by putting something definitive before them that they can try to achieve. How do you show a person struggling with the death of his grandfather for an entire movie? How will you know if he succeeds? By showing them smiling at the end?

Obsession (1976), which was inspired by Hitchcock's *Vertigo (1958)*, is an example of a poorly constructed want. In the former movie, a business man is driven to despair when a botched ransom exchange results in the apparent death of his wife and daughter. For most of the film, he is despondent as he tries to deal with his loss. The writer tries to put a twist into the story by showing the man's business partner as the one behind the kidnapping. After a brief struggle, the tormented husband kills his former business partner. Regardless of this scene, the main goal of the protagonist is to get control over his grief, which is why the movie doesn't work.

Had the writer crafted the story so that the husband felt something was amiss about the kidnapping and wanted to find the truth, then the story may have worked. This is why there was a lot of tension that moved the story forward in *Taken (2008)*. A father is trying to get his daughter back, not just dealing with his grief over her loss.

Stories are about emotion, but any story that has a person focusing solely on their own hardship or inner turmoil will run out of energy quickly. You can use the emotion as a base point to propel the story forward. *The Pursuit of Happyness (2006)* showed a single father trying to make a good life for his son. There were moments where he was down on his luck and all seemed lost. But, that's not what the story was about. Had it only dwelled on his emotional baggage, it never would've made it past page ten. Instead, the hardship was the catapult for a much larger story in terms of perseverance, dedication, sacrifice, and love for his child.

Second, the want in any story has to be simple. In the "grandfather" example, there was too much going on. The want has to be clean and concise.

I count myself among the very rare breed of males in the world who enjoy beer. A friend of mine fancied himself a brew master from the beer making kit he'd work with on weekends. One day, he handed me a large brown bottle of his latest brew for me to sample. After chilling it for a day, I poured it into a frosted mug and took a sip. It went down hard. The next two sips weren't any easier. The flavor was something along the lines of a stout, with hints of a wheat beer and it finished with the flavor of hops. He had attempted to put too many flavors into one beer. For those of you who don't indulge in beer, try chewing mint gum then immediately downing a glass of orange juice. You'll get the idea.

Again, the want needs to be simple: "A man wants to win over the girl of his dreams." "A woman wants to go back to school so she can be a nurse." "A father wants to reunite with his daughter." This last want sums up the film, *About Schmidt (2002)*. The catapult for his adventure is the unexpected death of his wife. But the want is *not* about coming to terms with her death.

Why does the want need to be so simple? You can only touch on so many points in a story. While the want may be brief, that doesn't necessarily translate to a one-track story. This is what confuses many writers. There is a belief that a huge, grandiose goal that the protagonist embarks on will lead to a fantastic screenplay.

Luke Skywalker wanted to leave his planet and become a Jedi Knight. What started as a simple want in *Star Wars (1977)* spawned the most recognizable film franchise in the world. Realize that from a simple want, other aspects of your protagonist will emerge. Luke's quest forces him to confront feelings of revenge, tests his loyalty, and often times isolates him from others.

Third, the goal has to be universal. Another problem with wants associated only with intangible emotional desires is that they aren't universal. Chances are, if you have a simple want, it will be something that everyone can appreciate. Luke Skywalker's want taps into our childhood fantasies. At some point, we've all wanted to run off to change the world for the better. The movie *Taken* taps into our primal need about avenging the wrongs against us. *Man on Fire (2004)*, *Munich (2005)*, the "Die Hard" franchise, all of these films have the audience walking away saying, "If that was me, I would've done the same thing."

Romantic-Comedies tap into the ideals of courtship and love that all of us nurture. This is especially true when they are based on the "boy meets girl, boy loses girl, boy gets girl back" formula. Who hasn't had a love in their life that slipped away, but we never forgot them? The template may be the same, but that simple want can be reused in so many different ways.

There is saying that it is better to tell a simple story well, then a complex one poorly. As you are crafting the want of your main character, you can tell if you are trying to make it complex if you have an "and" in your description.

Let's look at the example used earlier in this chapter. "He wants to reunite with his old girlfriend *and* go off to the military so he can make something of himself..." Stop just before the "and." Make the story about a man trying to reunite with his girlfriend. It's tangible, simple, and universal. That is what your story is about. The man can still try to go into the military, but that aspect of the story will be tied into him wanting to get his girlfriend back. How will that affect their relationship? Will that force him to make a hard choice?

The final point concerning the want is that it has to be in proportion to their status in life. Let's focus on the aspect of a man about to go into the military. If his character is coming from a privileged background, then what is really at stake? What is the worst that could happen if he doesn't get accepted? In *An Officer and a Gentlemen (1982)* the protagonist came from nothing. The iconic line of "I got no place to go!" sums up his entire life story.

For one contest, I read a script about a man who was trying to be a musician, but his father wanted him to go to law school. This created a win-win situation for the character, which is boring to the audience. There isn't far for the protagonist to fall. In *8-Mile (2002)* the main character is living in a trailer while trying to pick up shifts at the auto factory to avoid being evicted. The same theme is evident in *The Talented Mr. Ripley (1999), Rocky (1976),* and *Stand and Deliver (1988):* the classic rags-to-riches story.

However, not every story has to be that polarized. In the movie *Wall Street (1987)* if the main character weren't able to land the legendary Gecko, he would still have a job making a very comfortable living. But, in the context of that film, making $100,000 a year is synonymous with being poor. *Social Network (2010)* didn't engage you in the story because the protagonist was in danger of being on the street. No matter how much the main character would have to pay to settle lawsuit, he would still be one of the wealthiest men in the world. Instead, the story is about friendships and betrayal.

You can write scripts about industry titans and politicians with global power. To make them work, you create a universal want that everyone can understand. Very few of us would feel sympathetic about a billionaire who has to shell out a few million to settle a lawsuit. If you craft the story around a basic human element, then anyone can understand their plight.

Greek and Roman mythology still endure because they focus on the characters' fragile qualities. Zeus will never have to do his own laundry, but he is vulnerable to arrogance, narcissism, and is in fear of reprisal by his wife. *Citizen Kane (1941)* explores some very basic human elements that we all possess. The same goes for *The Aviator (2004)*, *Malcolm X (1992)* and *Amadeus (1984)*.

This chapter may seem a bit overwhelming because it explores the responsibility of the want. The takeaway point to all of this is that you shouldn't over-think what the main goal of your protagonist should be. Go with your instinct. Look to that first spark that inspired you to write the script. That is what your want should be about. If you have an idea about a girl from a small town who wants to make it as a big city lawyer, then stick with that as your want. Don't overcomplicate it. Your idea is already there: it's tangible, simple, and universal.

Sean Hinchey

CONFLICT

Now that you have a firm grasp as to what is expected of your characters regarding their **want** or **goal,** we can move onto another aspect that is tied directly into the want. Just as a story requires a want, it also needs **conflict.** Without a solid, well-defined conflict, the story will fall flat.

The simplest way to figure out what the conflict of your story should be is by thinking in terms of an **anti-want**. If your protagonist wants to save the world, then the conflict has to be that something or somebody won't allow that to happen. Here's how you can create fantastic conflicts for your protagonist.

First, just as some writers are unable to create a clear and plausible want, they are equally incapable of crafting a solid conflict. Why is that? Most writers are unaware that the purpose of having a story is to have the main character, or protagonist, put through a series of tests. Contest judges want to witness their struggle. The more setbacks and successes you can create, the better your story will be.

Every film that you've seen has conflict. Most documentaries do as well. We see the obstacles that life has thrown at a real-life person and we get to see how they transformed themselves.

In the film *School Ties* (1992) we are introduced to a man who plays football for a prestigious private school in the 1950s. However, he comes from a working-class family and is Jewish. The reason his story is interesting is that he doesn't fit into the old money crowd and he has to deal with the anti-Semitic slurs, since they all assume he comes from a WASP background like themselves.

Because he is the round peg going into the square hole, we are drawn to him. What inner resources does he have to resort to in order to play their game? Why does he subject himself to their world? If we were to focus on any of the other privileged students at the school, their story wouldn't be nearly as compelling.

In action movies, the conflict is always much clearer. There is one person representing the good guy who is trying to stop the bad guy from hurting other people. But what about Romantic-Comedies, do they have conflict?

Absolutely, one person is trying to win the affections of another. Somewhere in the background, there's a third party that is trying to stop this from happening. It could be an ex-husband or a former girlfriend or even the popular kid at school. Because it is a comedy, the conflict is handled in a much more humorous fashion. It's proportional to the story that is at hand. You won't find any gun play or extreme violence in these films because the tone of the story doesn't allow for that type of action. Conversely, in an action movie, you won't find the protagonist and the villain playing *rochambeau* to decide who the victor is.

Just as the want needs to be tangible, so does the conflict. Make sure that the conflict is something that puts the want of the main character in jeopardy. This could be in the form of psychological mind games; it doesn't always have to be physical.

The film *Enemy of the State* (1998) has our protagonist on the run based on a simple phone call made by the antagonist. Without even having to leave his desk, one man has managed to almost erase another person from the face of the earth. In other films, such as psychological thrillers, it's a matter of the protagonist figuring out what the other person knows. This creates a fragile game of chess. At any time either person can give away too much and could end up losing what they are trying to get. In *North by Northwest (1959)*, a regular man is whisked into international intrigue and has to find out who is behind it so he can escape alive.

Whatever the conflict is, make it simple and have it be present in every scene. While the protagonist and antagonist don't have to be facing off in every scene, the menace to the main character should be present. There needs to be a sense that at any given moment, the hero of the story could lose it all.

Keep the conflict aimed directly at the protagonist at all times. It's easy in the course of the story to have the villain veer off and begin antagonizing other people. That was the problem with *Spider-Man (2002)*. The Green Goblin managed to kill everyone who wronged him, then he let his anger loose on the city. Spiderman got caught in his crosshairs. The conflict never really made sense because it wasn't focused like a laser beam.

Ironman 2 (2010) had a problem with the conflict because the two antagonists were scheming to get back at Ironman. There wasn't enough head-to-head battling. The entire film was a buildup to a marginal climax. It never felt like Ironman was in danger for the bulk of the story.

Some examples of inner conflict manifesting itself are films such as *American Beauty (1999)*. The main character is in a loveless marriage, but his main conflict comes with his dissatisfaction with himself. He is stuck in a meaningless job, his wife is having an affair, and his only daughter refuses to talk to him. This definitely fulfills the requirement of having the conflict deal directly with the protagonist.

However, a common pitfall that writers fall into when addressing the man-versus-self conflict is that the story turns into a self-pity party. While there is a time for a character to lament, the story needs to be about the character changing. Can the character renew a relationship with her spouse or engage with her child? This theme has been utilized to great success in films such as *Ordinary People (1980)* and *About Schmidt (2002)*.

Conflict can be illustrated in many different ways. It can mean the end of world, as portrayed in most Science Fiction films, or it can be a man in search of his bike, as in *Bicycle Thieves (1948)*. Crafting a solid conflict that is opposite of the protagonist's want will catch the attention of the contest judge. Keep it simple, focused and make sure that it is evident in every scene. That's the key to writing like a professional.

Sean Hinchey

ACT I: GREAT OPENINGS

Screenplays follow a structure that can be found in every produced movie. If done properly, the structure blends seamlessly into the background. A screenplay is broken down into **Three Acts**. Act One takes up roughly 25% of the screenplay, Act Two is 50%, with the remaining 25% left for Act Three. As I read your script, I am very conscious of the act breaks.

If you have a one hundred-page script, I am expecting the main character to be catapulted in act two around page twenty five. If your script is running long in the second act and you only have ten pages left for your final act, there isn't enough time to resolve your conflict.

Many writers are set on breaking the rules. They are going to tell their story their way, and they won't be boxed in by some arbitrary rules designed to limit them. Here's the deal: The rules aren't designed to block anyone's writing. In a way, screenwriting rules were never really designed, they just came about.

Think about how you tell stories. If you relayed a funny story to your friends, you would set up the location of where it happened and describe the people involved. Then, you would tell the bulk of what was going on. Finally, you would reveal the punch line, the funny event that made the story memorable. Without even realizing it, you shared an event in a three act structure. It's how we communicate naturally: set it up, tell the story, and reveal the resolution.

For the writers out there who are still focused on breaking the rules, you shouldn't break them until you've mastered them. So, let's get started.

For each script, there is a beginning, a middle and an end. Sounds basic, almost insultingly simple, doesn't it? However, it's amazing how many writers who submit their work to screenwriting contests fail to really grasp this concept. The first act is the beginning to your entire story.

When you start, you are creating a new world from nothing. Your empty sheet of paper or blank computer screen is a canvas that hasn't been touched just yet. It's a new frontier and it's your job to properly prepare the contest judge for the ride you are about to take them on. For an opening act, there is a lot you have to accomplish. In the first act, you have to establish what your story is about. How do you go about doing this?

Create the time period that your story will reside in: past, present, or future. This can be done by establishing the surroundings, from the types of vehicles and style of clothes to the iconic buildings. This may sound very simplistic, but it is amazing how many scripts fail to establish the proper time frame. I refer to this as the **flavor.** It's like ordering dessert at a restaurant. Do you want something chocolate? Dense like a cake, or smooth and creamy like mousse? Perhaps you want something cold like ice cream or warm like flan.

Establish the flavor of your film. For films taking place in the present, this can be done rather easily. However, care needs to be taken so that a contest judge understands if we are in a big city, a small city, or a town. A contest judge is picking up your script and needs to align themselves with your world. However, this does not mean that you must describe everything down to the last detail. Just provide enough flavor so that the judge can get comfortable with the setting of your story.

Your protagonist needs to be revealed within the first ten pages of your script. Most stories have them present in the first scene, but that's not necessary. It's possible to set up some of the conflict in the first scene, so we can understand what the lead character will be up against in this story.

Most scripts spend too much time setting up the world, the conflict, and the secondary characters, but in that case, we don't see the protagonist until too late in the script. Who this character is also ties into your theme. Are they good, not so good, evil but redeemable? More will be discussed about characters in later chapters.

Finally, you need to make it clear what the story is about by letting us know what the character is trying to achieve, through the **want** or **goal**. As you are developing the character early on, you are also developing what their goal is: the two complement each other.

All of these elements need to be established in the first 25% of your script. This is the foundation of your story. You can't build a good story if the starting point is shaky.

At the end of this act, something happens that pushes the main character back to a point **below** where they were in the beginning of the story. In other words, everything was going fine for them, until an event happens that rattles their reality.

Star Wars (1977) opens with a huge battle that effectively sets up the world we are going to experience. Even in the script, George Lucas clearly establishes this alternate reality. Shortly after this battle sequence, which reveals the villain Darth Vader to us, we meet Luke Skywalker. What does Luke want? To join the rebellion and be a Jedi

Knight like his father.

He's unsure how he will go about this. Then fate steps in and changes his life. Luke arrives home and sees that his aunt and uncle are dead and learns that somebody is looking for him. At that exact moment, the first act has ended and we are now entering a new reality.

You will successfully catapult your protagonist into the second act by properly crafting your world and creating a great setback for your protagonist. Fracture the world that they know, so there is no going back for your protagonist.

The first ten pages of your script are very important, so make them pop. Instead of slowly setting up your story and preparing the reader for your character, jump right into the story and show us something interesting about your protagonist. It's like jumping into a cold swimming pool instead of dipping your toe in.

Ten pages is equivalent to ten minutes of screen-time. How much time do you give a film on DVD to capture your attention before you decide to watch something else? Most people have made up their mind within that time frame. *Road to Perdition (2002)*, *Avatar (2009)*, and *Get Him to the Greek (2010)* all have fantastic openings. Everything required in the first act is set up perfectly, which leaves us ready and eager to see the protagonist struggle in the next act.

It's astounding how many contest submissions fail at properly framing these crucial points in a screenplay. Hit them all in the right order, and the judge will be impressed from the outset with the structure of your story.

ACT II: THE VAST DESERT

The Second Act of a screenplay, the middle part, may be referred to as the vast desert because it's where many writers allow their protagonist to wither and die. This is the bulk of where you storytelling takes place. It's here that your character wanders around in search of meaning, in the crucible where they will be tested once the world of Act One is left behind.

The term "world" alludes to the reality that is created in your story. For example, you can have a small town where everyone knows each other. If someone in the town is murdered, that world is no longer the same. This does not mean that the small town, with all of its buildings, trees and parks, has to change physically.

What is the purpose of the second act? The main character has to go about his journey actively seeking what he wants. There will be other characters in the story whose purpose is to either help or hinder your hero's quest. But everything that happens is in relation to the goal.

What often happens in the course of this act is that the writer strays from the main storyline. For example, one contest submission featured a man trying to make it as a musician. He had very little money, barely a place to live but was determined to break into this difficult market. The first act starts off by setting up his dilemma, followed by a nice setback that catapulted the character into the second act.

It's was in the second act that the story unraveled. Instead of focusing on his music career, the script took a turn and we saw him in different relationships with women while he partied the nights away. While it is fine for him to interact with other people, how he deals with them should be in relation to his musical dreams, his want.

How can you make sure that your second act is properly structured and effectively moves the story forward? Follow these **Three Secrets** and you'll craft a solid second act.

First, make sure that you properly bridge the characteristics of your protagonist from the first act into the second act. In other words, if your character is trying to be a musician in the first act, don't have him suddenly try his hand at becoming a mechanic or a salesman.

The exception to this rule is if he has to do these jobs to pay bills in order to pursue his dream. In the film *Cinderella Man* (2005), we see a boxer who has to take a job in a warehouse moving around dry goods so he can feed his family. This doesn't mean he has given up on his dream or is trying to have a new career. His focus is still on boxing; the job is a necessity.

Suppose the writers of *Cinderella Man* had too many scenes of him performing odd jobs as an attempt to hammer home this desperation? The story would take a turn, and the dream of becoming a prizefighter would wither. In the example about the musician, the story transformed into something else. The relationships he formed took the focus *away* from his dream to be a successful musician. This leads me to ask, why even establish him as a musician to begin with?

How do you make sure that this doesn't happen in your screenplay? This takes us to the second secret. When re-reading your screenplay, make sure that every scene, particularly in the second act, is about what the main character wants. However, not every scene needs to be something positive. Think of your screenplay as an ocean. There are waves on the surface that flow to the beach, and an undertow they goes back out to sea. The protagonist is floating on top of these waves. They get closer to the shore, then pulled further away. In the second act, they never actually touch the beach.

It's this ebb and flow that makes for an exciting and dynamic second act. Where most screenplays fail is that the story becomes too static. The characters aren't doing much in relation to what the story is about: the want. To be clear, the people who populate your story can be performing the most exciting actions known to mankind, but if they don't relate to the goal, it won't work.

A common mistake is that writers feel they can create filler scenes to tide the story over until the third act happens. Without a solid second act, there won't be anybody around to see your final act.

No scene should ever be written as filler. Every scene and every line of dialogue must be germane to telling the story. The momentum is kept going by pushing the character toward their goal, then dragging them back. It's all about a cycle of success and failure that is repeated. Why is this the way a second act progresses?

It's never rewarding to see somebody simply get what they want. The story is about *how* they got it. Look at it this way: When a newspaper article has an exposé about a successful person, it usually starts off by introducing who they are now.

Maybe he is a real estate mogul, or she's CEO of a Fortune 500 company. As you read you begin to understand their back story. Maybe they started out in the mailroom of the company they are now in charge of. Perhaps they went to college at night, while they worked a menial job during the day.

It's this journey, the transformation of the individual, that makes for an interesting read. It's easy to see a person standing at the pinnacle of their success, but that image fades away rather quickly. It's the struggle that endears us to them and makes their story relevant and interesting.

The third secret to writing a solid second act is to recognize that you are writing something that will create a movie-going experience for the audience. The concept of an experience is something that most contest entries seem to overlook. What do we mean by experience? The second act needs to be crafted in a manner that draws the reader into your world. Many scripts tend to ramble on with facts that would play more into a documentary format than a screenplay.

For example, if a person suffers a great setback in achieving his goal, it's better for us to *see* it than to *hear* about it. Writers tend to gloss over the negative, difficult parts of the protagonist's life. Instead, they rush to show us how he succeeded. But success can only be measured in relation to failure.

In *Braveheart (1995)*, we see the main character involved in many battles where he leads men who believe in him to their deaths. As the audience, we get to feel his charismatic power over the men, but we also get to see him as a man. The most poignant scene is when he is betrayed by a person he trusts. The protagonist's reaction to the betrayal is evident, and in that moment we see him for what he is: a simple man, not a god. The impact wouldn't have been as powerful if we saw two men talking about the protagonist's betrayal. While crafting such scenes is difficult, it is precisely those moments that make the story worth reading. There are no shortcuts.

Another great example is in *Wall Street (1987)*, when the house of cards is falling down around our main character. We witness his rise to the top of his game in the stock market, then see everything crumble. The main character's arrest at the end has us feeling bad for him because we were part of his entire journey.

Again, don't resort to *explaining* the conflict or the setbacks. Create a movie experience; allow the audience to feel as if they are watching something happen that they aren't supposed to. It's like being at a party where something unusual happens. When you are there, you are part of the group experience. If you didn't make it and hear about it later, it's just not the same. It's one of those "had to be there" moments. Never write scenes in the second act that leave the reader on the outside. They are your party guests.

Involving the audience isn't always about special effects, dazzling gun play, or car chases. Going back to the voyeur aspect of the audience, it's about pulling back the curtain and letting the viewer in for a peek. *Rope (1948)* takes place in one location, an apartment. But there is so much tension that the audience feels like they are a fly on the wall for the entire story and they can't turn away from what is happening.

While the first act sets up the story, it's the second act where the audience really *lives*. They are settled into the plot and are absorbing the ebb and flow of the character's journey. At the end of this act, something has to happen where the main character is pushed back further than they have ever been before. It creates a seemingly impossible situation where all hope is lost. From this rock bottom place, the reader witnesses the true and genuine characteristics of the protagonist. From that point forward, all lies and veneers are stripped away. What we will witness in the final act is their true persona.

An effective way of setting up their downfall is by having their best laid plans laid waste. In *Outland (1981)* we see our protagonist stash weapons in hidden areas around the space colony. When the time comes for the main character to confront the hit-men sent to kill him, he finds that all his weapons have been removed. It doesn't matter who took them. The scene illustrates that the protagonist is outgunned and possibly outsmarted. How can he get the upper-hand on the situation? In *Gladiator (2000)*, a man loyal to the protagonist offers up an escape plan. When the main character manages to flee his prison, the loyal man is found hanged and our hero is surrounded by his enemy.

In the final scenes of this act, you should be changing the expectations of what the reader thinks will happen in the final act. If you show the hero planting weapons to use later, then it's expected that they will be used. If the end happens exactly as it was planned, there's no surprise for the audience. That's why you remove the weapons. Forcing the character to think of a new way out of the situation reveals their resourcefulness. This keeps your character out of their comfort zone right up until the very end.

The second act can be a very difficult act because there is so much information that needs to be revealed. Don't be in a rush to get through the scenes. This is the core of

Sean Hinchey

the journey you are taking the character through. Never look at this act as a nuisance. Many submissions have a good first act with a well crafted setup. Then the writer glosses over the second act just so they can get to the climax of the story.

Without an effective second act, the climax will be meaningless. You want the contest judge to cherish every scene and to be riveted to every aspect of your story.

SIGNIFICANT DETAILS

Before we work through the obstacles of crafting a solid completion to your screenplay-the Third Act-it's vital to understand the effective use of **significant details**.

While it is possible to discuss the third act structure without talking about significant details, it doesn't work the other way around. The significant detail can only be fully explored by understanding how it comes to fruition in the final act.

What is a significant detail? To paraphrase the playwright Anton Chekov, if you show a rifle in the beginning of your story, it must be shot by the end. This is referred to as "Chekov's Gun." Never spend time developing any specific detail if it isn't relevant to the story. This isn't to say that you should expunge any and all descriptions in your script. But, if you focus the attention of the judge on a pickup truck's loose rear bumper, then that bumper better fall off, cause an accident, and change the course of the entire story.

Sometimes the term **throwaway** is used. A throwaway was planted in the beginning act of *Things Change* (1988) when the main character received a twenty-five cent piece from a mafia don to be used if the man ever got in trouble. It's this exact quarter that saves his life at the end of the film. The quarter seems trivial at first, like a detail that you can throw away, but in the end it proves pivotal to the story.

In *The Fifth Element (1997)* we see the protagonist trying to light a cigarette while he is on the phone, but there is only one match left—which he saves for later-and it ends up saving the world.

Sean Hinchey

When you are crafting your story, it's important to be very sparing with your description, as we've talked about. If you are focusing on something specific, make sure it comes into play by the final act of the story. You won't see a throwaway come into focus and then not be used in the final act of any produced film. Why is that? The screenplay will have gone through many rewrites by the time a single frame of film is shot. There aren't any examples of how *not* to use a throwaway in an existing movie.

An example from a contest submission established a woman that wore a specific red dress at certain points in the film. While the description didn't go into great detail about the style of it, the color "red" was made perfectly clear as the story progressed. Would the payoff be something along the lines of the glasses of water left through the house in the film *Signs* (2002)? I was expecting something important to happen at the end that would tie in the dress, a touchstone moment that would bring the story together. Nothing happened. I knocked off points for that wild goose chase.

Again, this isn't to suggest that you avoid descriptions in all of your scenes. But, make sure that the descriptions are concise and relatively vague, unless you are calling attention to a specific detail. Many writers describe too many unimportant items in great detail, creating the expectation that everything will pay off. To try to make everything important is to make nothing important. Detailed description of a specific item is a way of saying, "Focus on this, remember it, because it will come into play later."

In *Darkman* (1990) there's a scene where the protagonist sets his coffee cup on an important document that his girlfriend is looking at, leaving a coffee ring. Later in the story, he sees that same piece of paper and is able to understand how the attack on his girlfriend and himself is tied together. It's a very brief moment that seems like a very minor, innocent mistake. That throwaway was an important part in the story.

If I were reading the script and the writer focused on that moment, as a judge I would expect there to be some tie-in later on. Why else would the writer insert a line about the coffee cup leaving a ring on an important document?

Many screenplays have descriptions about a character throwing a letter with their address on it in a garbage pail, or they leave the car keys above the driver's side visor, or forget their cell phone in a restaurant. All of these events would leave anyone reading the script to believe that this will have some relevance to the story.

All significant details need to be worked into the first act. It's like planting seeds that will bear fruit later in the story. There's no rule regarding how many you can have in a script. However, they need to count for something, by either helping or hindering the protagonist on their journey.

Significant details show that you are a smart writer, not merely a clever one.

ACT III: GREAT ENDINGS

The third and final act to your screenplay is full of many pitfalls. While lots of script submissions have their share of issues with the second act, it's astounding the number of screenplays that fall to pieces in the final act. While your writing needs to be solid for the entire length of your script, a truly dazzling Act Three will allow you to finish in style. It's like having a memorable dessert after a great meal.

The third act is the capstone to your entire screenplay, so it needs to be fantastic and it must be logical. Every script must have these **Three Key Points** in the third act.

First, there is nothing more that we can learn about the main character in the story regarding his abilities. This is not to be confused with any twist in the story, and we will explore this difference. If you have a protagonist who enters a building to confront another person, you cannot have that person utilize abilities that we haven't seen before.

For example, if you have a woman who works as a bartender confronting a person holed up inside an apartment with a gun, you have to maintain the reality of who your protagonist is. The bartender isn't going to launch into surreal karate moves or produce a bazooka to dispatch the bad guy. Unless you've established that the bartender is skilled in the martial arts, this won't work.

The bartender, skilled at understanding personality types from working behind a bar for years, may engage in a game of wits. She may be able to spot a weakness in the person that could be exploited to gain the upper hand and quash the situation.

You can have a character with a simmering rage that builds for the entire story. That is the moment where a "mild-mannered man" simply snaps as in *Straw Dogs* (1971), *John Q* (2002), or *Falling Down* (1993). But if your character performs a feat which requires cunning, strength, or other resources not apparent in the rest of the story, then the ending will come off as contrived. Any twist that you have in the final act of your screenplay has to be based on the information we already know.

A contest-submitted screenplay had a man scaling a cliff by climbing a rope to get to his objective. The ease with which he overcame the obstacle was disjointed. There was nothing in the story to suggest that he was in any great physical shape or had the knowledge of how to master the art of extreme rock climbing. The reason it didn't work was that the man embarked on the journey from the bottom of the cliff with all of the proper equipment.

However, if that same man had been pushed off the cliff and managed to grab onto the rope and pull himself up, that would work. It would show a strong survival instinct on his part. There is a difference between actively climbing the cliff versus reactively trying to save himself.

The second point dealing with the final act is that you have to wrap up the conflict. One contest submission was a drama about two men who grew up together in a small town. One man went away, but he came back to visit ten years later. As the two men catch up on old times, they realize how different their lives may have been if they weren't bullied by a jock in high school. They decide to get back at him, since the former bully never left the small town.

The problem with the story was that we only saw the

bully in two scenes up until the final act. At the end of the story, we see the two men reluctantly beating up their former tormentor. The ending didn't work because the majority of the story focused on these two men trying to relive the good old days. The bully, who was supposed to be the source of their conflict, was never developed.

This created an unsatisfying ending. Had the bully turned out to be a nice guy, there would've been some mixed emotions about punishing someone for the transgressions of the past. If the bully were still a bad person, there might've been a feeling of redemption. The writer set up a possible conflict and thought that it would somehow survive all the irrelevant twists and turns that the story took. Conflict is like a living creature that needs to be nurtured and tended to so that it can flourish.

Very often in Romantic-Comedies, we see one person trying to win the affections of another. What usually happens is that the romantic interest dwindles as the story progresses, and we see very little of the other person for the majority of the script. Instead, we see the protagonist in funny situations, or they are trying to get their life back on track. Either way, the romance gets lost in all this background noise.

By the final act, we see the two people together in a scene where they profess their love for each other. The story ends with the two of them about to embark on a blissful life together. This ending never works. The story is supposed to be about the two people generating a romantic spark, having it fizzle, then watching them rekindle the romance.

The trap that writers fall into is that they believe a Romantic-Comedy has to have a lot of funny moments.

While this is true, all of those scenes have to be primarily about the romance. It's not enough for the story just to be funny.

Resolving the conflict in any screenplay is what the audience has paid their money to see. They've witnessed the character setup, and they've seen the protagonist get bounced around. The final act decides if that person will get what they want or go home empty handed. The resolution of the conflict needs to be a natural progression of all the events leading up to that moment.

The third and final key point of the third act is that the main character has to have changed. There is an exception to this that will be discussed later. The purpose of a screenplay is to take the audience on a journey of transformation. There are an innumerable ways that the protagonist can be altered by the conclusion of the story. He may be a little wiser, overcome a great fear, or he can accept responsibility for actions resulting in someone else's loss.

Their entire journey of overcoming conflict comes at a price. In the chapter about the first act, we discussed how the character encounters a setback that alters the world he knew and is set on a course that will forever change him. This change is permanently set by the end of the final act, which is the end of the story.

Without this change, the conflict in the story may be satisfied, but the overall character arc is stagnated. The change on the part of the character should be in proportion to the conflict. If the story is about a boy trying to win the heart of a girl he's always had a crush on, then it would make sense for him to feel more confident by the end of the film. Someone conquering an evil empire and saving the world would have a much larger change of character.

This isn't to suggest that figuring out this change should keep you up at night. It should be something organic and logical in terms of your story. If your character started off at Point A, they will go through a series of successes and setback by the time they reach Point Z. What would be the proper mindset for the character to have by the end of the story?

It's something that is very easy to create and illustrate to the contest judge, yet many writers fail to give any thought to this aspect. While this detail won't sink your entire screenplay, if other scripts have successfully tackled this issue, it may push yours further to the bottom of the pile.

Now we can discuss the exception to the rule saying that the protagonist must change. Very simply, if the main character in your story is the same at the end of the script as they were at the beginning, then everyone else in the story must be affected. An example of this is *Law Abiding Citizen* (2009). The protagonist witnesses a horrific crime against his family and vows revenge on everyone in the legal system who didn't bring all the criminals to justice. The protagonist is just as evil by the end of the story-he hasn't changed. However, the other people in the story have changed. They've questioned their decisions and are reflecting on their culpability in the situation. In the context of this film, it wouldn't work if the protagonist suddenly has a change of heart. He is too set on vengeance. For him to have an epiphany and realize the error of his ways would come across as too contrived.

Finally, when you reach the climax of your story-the main character gets what they want-your story is over.

You can have one more wrap up scene, something like an epilogue. But, you need to end your screenplay: The End. *Lord of the Rings: The Return of the King (2003)* had us witnessing the evil ring being thrown into the lava. That sequence alone was painfully long. After that, the movie continued for another thirty minutes.

At the end of *Star Wars (1977)*, Luke blew up the Death Star, then landed his fighter. The final scene was of him and his friends getting an award. The credits rolled and everyone got to go home. When it's over, it's over.

The third act has a lot of requirements to make it work right. If the first act presents you with a box of dominos, the second act has you setting them up and the final act is when you knock them down. How they fall makes the difference between a good script and a great one.

KEY POINTS

- Without a solid want, the audience has nothing to engage them in the story.

- The want needs to appeal to everyone, so it should be simple and universal.

- The conflict is the anti-want; it needs to be aimed directly at the protagonist.

- Conflict needs to be in proportion to the tone of your story.

- Act One has to set up your characters, the want, and the conflict.

- A major setback is required to push the protagonist into the second act.

- Act Two is the bulk of your storytelling, so don't be in a rush to get through it.

- The main character should always be pushed toward or pulled away from his goal in the second act.

- If you focus on a specific physical item in the story, make it relevant to the protagonist's outcome.

- Layer in the significant detail in the first act so that the audience forgets about it, until it's needed.

- In Act Three, when you've reached the climax of your screenplay, your story is over.

- The protagonist needs to have changed by the end of the story. If he doesn't, then those around him need to be affected.

FOUR: CHARACTERS

DEFINING YOUR PROTAGONIST

Characters need to be well-developed in order to grab the attention of the contest judge. When they aren't, they are "two-dimensional" or "cardboard cutouts." When they are great, they are "fully fleshed out." What they do in the script is what propels the story forward. There are limits and possibilities when it comes to crafting solid characters. The journey they make from the beginning to the end is referred to as their "arc." Make your characters real and a judge will be turning the pages with zeal.

The protagonist is the "good guy" in your screenplay that we will be following. The entire story is about their journey, as they go about getting what they want.

Many contest submissions lose track of their main character. The story veers into the lives of the secondary characters or the antagonist-the "bad guy." While the secondary characters are important to the storytelling, they cannot overshadow the story of the protagonist.

In one Romantic-Comedy, the focus of the story shifted to the protagonist's best friend. While there were some funny moments in this person's life, it was unclear what was happening with our main character, which created a very disjointed ending. How do you keep your story on track by focusing solely on your main character? Realize that everything that this person does will either be an action or reaction to what is happening in the world around him.

Luke Skywalker in *Star Wars (1977)* wanted to become a Jedi Knight. For him to achieve that goal, he had to leave his planet and go on an **active** journey to seek out the training and experience he would need. This action is in direct relation to his **want.** Every action that Luke takes has to be in order to further this goal. As he progresses through this story, events unfold that challenge Luke. We then witness him **react** to what is happening. How any character overcomes the challenges before them will help define who they are as a character.

A major problem appearing in contest submissions is that the protagonist mostly reacts to events around him. In other words, we see him bump around the script while the secondary characters force the protagonist this way and that way.

In *Night Shift* (1982) the main character is about to be married to a woman with severe social issues, while he is stuck in a night job at a morgue. Throughout the film, he is pushed and pulled in different directions. However, he actively tries to gain control of his life, which often times results in failure. If he were to only react to the events around him, we would lose sympathy for the character and the story would be stale.

There isn't any set ratio of how much a character should actively try to change the events versus react to the world around him. The key to remember is that your character will have a certain natural rhythm you will discover that is unique to him. A quiet desk type person might be a bit more passive than a take-charge personality such as those in *Gladiator* (2000) or *The Last Castle* (2001).

How are the uses of dialogue and description used to further expose your protagonist?

When crafting your character, focus on what you want

to show the audience and what you want to tell them. In general, it's better to show what your protagonist is capable of. There are times where it simply isn't practical. Maybe it was something that happened to your character in the past and you don't want to resort to a flashback.

Unforgiven (1992) focuses on a man who is trying to redeem himself. We see that he can handle himself, but much of what we learn about him is from what others say about this mysterious man. By the end of the film, we learn that he was once a ruthless man and it is summed up when he says, "I've killed just about everything that walks or crawled at one time or another." Since this film is about a redeemed man trying to shake off his checkered past, the layering in about his previous life works well.

If the film were about a bad man doing even worse things, then we would want to see him performing heinous acts. The visual of his downward slide would be very powerful. In *Unforgiven*, hearing about William Munny's sordid past makes it that much scarier. The man looks trustworthy, but he hides a very dark soul. Some might consider this character to be an anti-hero, which is discussed in the next chapter. However, he falls into the gray area of the *reluctant hero*.

This is the person who wants to be left alone but is drawn into a situation and reluctantly does the right thing. Sean Connery's character in *Finding Forrester (2000)* doesn't want to get involved in an aspiring writer's life, preferring to remain a recluse. *Sexy Beast (2000)* has a great reluctant hero because the main character is pulled into a heist that he has no interest in. Once he is strong-armed by other people, it's fine for him to do what he has to in order to get his life back.

Understand that when characters talk, they may not always tell the truth. They say one thing, but do something completely different. In *Less Than Zero* (1987) we see a drug-addicted youth talk about opening up the hottest night club in Los Angeles. In reality, his life is a mess. He loses track of time, is in debt to his dealer, and has hurt everyone close to him. This is an example of what they say and who they really are, being in conflict. The dialogue, in this example, would have him spouting out about his grandiose dreams. In the screenplay description, we would see him asleep on a park bench in the same clothes that he had on the previous night. This illustrates the disconnect between the words that the character speaks and how things actually are.

There are limitations to screenwriting, such as not being able to read what a person is thinking, as one would in a novel. This can be overcome by the use of voice-over, the pitfalls of which I discussed earlier. However, since voice-over should be used sparingly, how does a writer get across what the main character is thinking?

One effective way of allowing us to peek into the mind of the protagonist is by using lean descriptions of their actions. For example, if two old friends meet up at an event after years of not seeing each other, they may exchange pleasantries. The main character may have a smile plastered on their face. As soon as the other person turns to leave, the smile drops. That would tell the contest judge that there is bad history between these two.

Little clues like that go a long way toward character development. As the story progresses, the contest judge will learn more and more about this person, which makes it interesting because not every detail is exposed at once.

Sean Hinchey

Character development doesn't have to happen all at once. In *Ironman* (2008) we think we know everything about the main character: he's smart, witty, good looking, rich, and is quite the ladies' man. In the second act, we realize that he is in fact very lonely and can only trust one person. If we learned everything about him in the opening scenes of the movie, we wouldn't be as engaged. Learning about the protagonist should be an evolution.

When a judge reads a script, it's as if they are going on a date with the main character. You want to learn a little bit as you go. For the most part, people put on their best face during the first couple of meetings. After a few dates, you learn a little bit about their weaknesses and vulnerabilities. That's what makes them human and, ultimately, likable.

Never rush the process of character development. Use the tools of dialogue and description to reveal the character's truths as well as his lies. When done properly, a well-developed character can seem like a real person. That's what makes for a successful script.

THE ANTI-HERO

Some screenplays use an **anti-hero** instead of the protagonist. What is an anti-hero? As the name suggests, they are the main character but they have less than desirable characteristics. There are flaws that don't make them purely evil; rather they make the reader unsure if we like them. Writing them can be a challenge, and very rarely in screenplay submissions are they well written.

The idea behind the anti-hero is that he does bad things. However, in relation to the people around him, he is a decent person. In *Payback (1999)* we catch glimpses of just how bad our main character is. Immediately, we don't like him. As the story progresses we understand that the people he is going up against aren't very nice either.

Because of this comparison, we give him the benefit of the doubt. He wants to get back the money stolen from him, and not one penny more. At one point in the story one of his victims is aghast that the anti-hero isn't demanding all the money, by saying, "70,000 dollars? I got suits that cost more than that!"

This anti-hero has a code which gives him a likable quality. He's willing to kill people to get back what was stolen from him, but he isn't about to get greedy. Since he was shot and left for dead when his money was stolen, we are willing to cut him some slack.

A great anti-hero creates a "better the devil you know than the devil you don't" scenario. In the film *The Professional (1994)* we are introduced to a hit man who lives as a recluse. By nature, hit men are bad people. Someone you probably wouldn't even want to know. In this film we learn that he wants to be left alone in his apartment so he can drink his milk. Something happens early in the story where a young girl, whose family has been brutally murdered, goes to the hit man's apartment for refuge. He reluctantly takes her in.

A young girl seeking help from a hit man seems like an unlikely match. However, we do know that he's a quiet man in contrast to the corrupt police officer out to get her. We breathe a sigh of relief that she is at least with someone that the audience knows. Chances are, he's not going to kill her since he only kills for money.

At this point, it's important to recognize that anti-heroes usually thrive in a violent setting. It would be hard to craft a likable anti-hero in any other world. In the world of *The Professional*, the contract killer is as nice as the people in this story are going to get.

The anti-hero has to have something redeemable about them. Our previously mentioned hit man has a major flaw, but he has a soft spot for the girl in trouble.

Road to Perdition (2002) has an anti-hero who is out to save his son. Even though he works for the Irish mafia, he makes sure that his loyalties lie with what's left of his family. Taken out of context, we wouldn't care if this anti-hero lives or dies; in fact we may want to see him dead. In this film, we want to see him exact his revenge so that his son can be free of the violence.

We develop similar feelings for our main character in *Layer Cake* (2004). Although the man is a drug dealer, he is trying to do one last score so he can get out of the business forever. It would be hard to create a likable character out of someone who makes a living getting people addicted to drugs. It works here because he is loyal to his friends, tries avoiding violence whenever possible, and is clearly in over his head.

In these examples, the writers capitalized on something very basic and universal about characters in general. They found a way to make us interested in unlikable people. By crafting a world in which the anti-hero is the most innocent of all the other characters, the writer taps into something genuinely human, and we find ourselves drawn into their story. Ultimately, we want anti-heroes to get what they want.

This issue was lacking in *The Town* (2010). The main character falls in love with a woman who is a witness to a robbery he engineered, at the bank where she works. Falling in love is a good mechanism to have in a screenplay, but it's not always enough to carry the whole story. The anti-hero is part of a team of men who have killed policemen, and we know he would do it again. It's hard to get around that kind of obstacle.

He does nothing to make amends for his actions. His loyalty to his crew is unwavering, but he never makes any demands that they ease off on the killing. That does little to endear us to the character. There is nothing in his dialogue or his actions to suggest that he has any intention of changing who he is.

Granted, he wants to do one last heist then get out of the crime business, but that doesn't mean he won't kill on this last job. Because the writer fails at creating a likable anti-hero, there is nothing in the story to root for. It's an unsatisfying ending because he is able to walk away, while the rest of his crew is killed. He doesn't get the girl at the end of the story, but that doesn't make him sympathetic, nor does it balance the scales for all the murders he was involved in.

The anti-hero needs to have some change affect him, while still remaining the same person. While this sounds contradictory, it really isn't when you parse the difference.

The anti-hero in *The Professional* opened the story as a hit man, and he died a hit man. Who he is as a person hasn't changed. He was trained to kill for money and to protect himself. However, he found a purpose in his life when he decided to protect an orphaned girl. The minute he opened the door to her, his life went on a *slightly* different path. He is partially redeemed.

Change is usually great for protagonists in other genres. Here, however, the character is altered in a more nuanced manner. Look at the anti-heroes in *Thank You For Smoking (2005), Man on Fire (2004), Pitch Black (2000), Cool Hand Luke (1967), Casablanca (1942)*, as a few examples. Are these people changed by the end of the story?

Anti-heroes are not nice people; they do not experience a complete change of character. What we should see in the story is a glimpse of humanity. It's a very intimate moment that is shared with the audience, a peek into what they are capable of becoming, but never quite attain.

It's not important if these people are truly evil at their core. They are trying to do what is necessary to survive in the circumstances, which is why the viewer can forgive them for many of their transgressions. A brief, selfless act solidifies this belief.

A well written anti-hero can launch a basic plot into an engrossing and complex story. They can be put into many settings and they can possess the attributes of both a protagonist and an antagonist.

Sean Hinchey

CREATING YOUR VILLAIN

Just as every screenplay has to have a solid protagonist in their screenplay, you need to have a great antagonist. For the purposes of this chapter, we will be focusing on crafting a worthy villain.

What is the difference between an antagonist and a villain? The antagonist is the person who will be trying to keep the protagonist from getting what they want. The want of the antagonist is directly opposite to the goal of the main character. If the "good guy" wants to get a promotion that comes with the corner office, the "bad guy" will do everything he can to sabotage it.

A villain is a more extreme version of an antagonist. Darth Vader is a villain. Bill Lumbergh, the coffee-drinking, TPS report obsessed boss in *Office Space (1999)* is an antagonist. While the terms are often times used interchangeably, the general usage is that a villain is involved in some very evil acts. Villains are also referred to as a nemesis.

In this chapter, we will discuss villains. If you know how to write a solid villain, you will have no problem reining in the tone for an even-tempered antagonist.

One of the greatest villains ever written for film is the role of Hans Gruber in *Die Hard (1988)*. While there are other fantastic villains out there which will be used as examples, Hans fulfills all the requirements of what it takes to be great.

Keep in mind as you read this chapter, contest judges *love* fantastic villains.

A villain needs to be charismatic. This means they can be witty and charming. These are the types of people who, for the most part, you wouldn't mind inviting home for dinner. If you were to dress Hannibal Lector, from *The Silence of the Lambs (1991)*, in a jacket and tie instead of his iconic head cage and furniture dolly, wouldn't he make a great cocktail party guest? His intelligence gives him a great aura, if you overlook the cannibalism. While Noah Cross in *Chinatown (1974)* may not be the best looking person you've seen, he had a presence. His personality exuded a certain quality that would draw you to him.

Intelligence is another very important factor. Intelligence can be very charismatic. If they aren't smart, they wouldn't be a successful villain for very long. This doesn't mean that they have to be a genius, just very good at what they do. A situational awareness of the environment that they are in gives them an edge. This doesn't mean that they would be a great villain in all situations. While Noah Cross may operate with impunity in 1930's Los Angeles, he may not fare so well as a villain in a Wild West film. They are very good in their setting.

Charisma for a villain means they have a certain way about them, a quiet sense of power, that other people respect and even fear. It doesn't matter how they got it. They have it now, and they are in charge. A great asset for a villain is that they don't have to yell to get their point across. The way they carry themselves speaks volumes about the power they wield.

A villain has to possess the ability to make you love to hate them. In every movie in the "Star Wars" franchise, Darth Vader is a formidable presence. He is cruel, arrogant and ruthless. Yet, you can't get enough of him.

Sean Hinchey

In *Live Free or Die Hard (2007)* the villain is so blatantly narcissistic that you want to strangle him. Yet, there's a sense of loss when he finally gets his justice at the end. This is how you want to affect the contest judge with your villain. You want your script pages to get wrinkled in their tightly-clutched hands as they read your script through gritted teeth thinking, "I can't stand this person...give me more!" If the judge is emotionally attached to your villain, you've done very well for yourself.

A great villain needs to have the authentic belief that what they are doing is correct. The character of William Stryker in *X-Men: X2 (2003)* is among the top ten villains of all time. This is a man who is filled with such hatred against the mutants that he is willing to do anything to wipe them out. This includes the sacrifice of his own son who has evolved into a mutant.

However, it's not a blind rage when he lashes out at everyone. Instead, he has managed to focus his energies into taking out the leaders of the mutants. His hatred has been channeled into a firm belief in his actions. In his mind, there is only right and wrong and he is firmly on the side of the just. When you have a character who is so morally warped, it draws the viewer in.

When we speak of any moral fracture, this is not about villains in the realm of horror porn. While slasher movies continue to make money, crafting a villain who simply preys on the horrific suffering of his victims takes very little imagination. To say that a character was unloved by his mother and therefore decides to dismember everyone with a hatchet does not require the subtle nuances of creating great villains.

Moral fractures or flexibilities are inherent in characters

such as The Joker in the "Batman" movies, the warden in *Shawshank Redemption (1994)*, or the neighbors in *Rosemary's Baby (1968)*. While some of these characters may be monstrous, the reasons for their evil misdeeds have a solid basis in the past. Their actions serve to tell a solid story, not to create shock value which becomes the story.

The villain should have a distinct advantage over the protagonist. This could be in the form of influence, money, intelligence, or sheer size. What the hero of the story does is try to utilize his resources to exploit the chink in the villain's armor. This does not mean that their specific skill sets have to be evenly matched.

Many contest submissions have villains that are a bit too weak to really challenge the main character. You want these two characters to go head to head, exchanging blows at every encounter. In *Die Hard (1988)* the villain had intelligence and a well-oiled team at his disposal. Our hero has the mindset of a police officer and the element of surprise. When writing your character, make each of their strengths and weaknesses different and unique. This is evident in sporting events. Each team has a strength that the other team is lacking. However, they have weaknesses which the opposing team will be able to exploit.

It's this combination of using your strong suit while adapting for the unknown that makes for great sparring throughout the film. The key here is not to give the villain and protagonist a huge arsenal of resources. A few special talents will do the trick; then set them loose on each other. In *Duplicity (2009)* the two heads of major corporations are waging battle on each other. In the end, one of the men plays on the other's arrogance:

his weak spot. Not everything needs to be about bigger guns, faster cars, or better martial arts skills.

A villain's want is in direct proportion to the main character's goal. What the protagonist wants and the villain is after are like goal zones on the opposite ends of the field. However, their clash will be somewhere in the middle.

For example, in *Michael Clayton* (2007) the main character is trying to save a friend from ruining his own career, which will also drag down the protagonist's career. The villain is trying to kill both of them. Each of their goals is in conflict, but the main battle doesn't take place on the edges, close to the goal. The clash is in the middle of the field and is the confluence of these two characters trying to fulfill their respective goals. Eventually both parties will get pushed to the fringe of the field, and someone will cross the goal line.

In many submissions, the writer pits the two people in conflict right at the line of demarcation. For example, a script had a man who was trying to kill off a farmer so he could get his land due to some unusual clause in the will of the original owner. The story was in the realm of *A Simple Plan* (1998). Right away, we see the villain trying to kill the other man who then defends himself.

The problem was that the story became this back and forth motion but with no tension, no finesse. The conflict needed to be established, then we should've seen the villain begin the plan to kill the farmer. By having a slow buildup, we would've gotten to know both characters better and there would've been a more organic conclusion to the situation. Metaphorically speaking, it's better to see the villain slap the protagonist, who returns the favor with a soft body blow. The back and forth escalates until it's a bloody fight. If both parties come out swinging full force, where can the story go from there?

Even in the James Bond films, the villain sizes up Bond to see if he's a threat and weigh the ramifications of killing the agent. Then, the battle of wits begins and the tension continues to escalate.

A great villain must create an emotional attachment with the reader or judge of the story. All of the other elements come down to this one point. The person reading your script has to despise, admire, envy, and yet be puzzled by your villain. One script I read had my mind worked up in such a froth over the villain that I pushed it to the finalist round even before I finished reading it. I couldn't get the character out of my head because of all the emotions it triggered in me.

That's what you should be seeking when you craft a quality villain. You want to tickle the universal negative emotions that they stir up in each of us. It's the desire for revenge that comes from a wide array of personal experiences. Maybe you've been unjustly fired from a job in the past, bullied in high school, humiliated by an ex-beau. The villain conjures up a past wrong that all of us have experienced, and allows the audience to see the bad guy get their comeuppance.

When writing an antagonist—one that isn't considered a villain—these emotions may be scaled back. However, most Romantic-Comedies have the arrogant guy/catty girl who is dating the object of affection for our protagonist. We love it when they are taken down a few notches by the end. An antagonist is "villain-light," but the reader still needs to experience an emotional attachment. If you

Sean Hinchey

make that kind of connection with the contest judge, you will get noticed, which often translates to winning.

SECONDARY CHARACTERS

Secondary characters are the forgotten heroes of many screenplays. They exist in the shadows of the more important characters: the protagonists and antagonists of the stories. Even though they may be minor players in the story, their role in moving the screenplay forward is enormous. When it comes time for the awards, they are known as the supporting actors.

The protagonist and antagonist usually do not exist in a story alone. There are exceptions to this rule. Some people may argue that Castaway (2000) had the protagonist on the island alone. However, the volleyball, Wilson, could be considered a secondary character, a source for the main character to confide in. Wilson also gave the protagonist a reason to talk so we could learn more about his plight.

Films such as Moon (2009), Sleuth (2007), and Hard Candy (2005) are very focused movies, in the sense that they only have one or two characters in the bulk of the film. Isolating these people goes to the crux of what the story is about. For this chapter, we'll be talking about the majority of movies that have many secondary characters.

Secondary characters help fill out the story. They give your concept a sense of space to operate in. As long as you are going to populate your script with other characters, you need to develop them. If not, these entities will come across as cardboard cutouts simply occupying space.

Even in I Am Legend (2007), the writer went to great lengths to establish the mannequins as characters. They wore different clothes, had names, and inhabited the video store that the protagonist visits to maintain a routine. Ironically, these inanimate characters had more depth to them than many secondary characters in contest-submitted scripts.

The purpose of these characters is to help or hinder the protagonist on his quest to get what he wants. The main character is king or queen in their story. What the protagonist wants to achieve relates to the actions of the secondary characters. If the guy wants to get the girl, his buddy has to either help them or get in their way of making it happen.

In *About Last Night (1986)* two people begin a romance amid their individual busy lives. The roommate of the main character doesn't approve of her friend's choice in men. Nor does she care for the friends this new boyfriend surrounds himself with. Through the ups and downs of this budding relationship, the secondary characters play a large role in helping to shape the course of their friends' lives. The secondary character can be a loyal follower, a mentor, a close friend, or someone who double-crosses the main character. Whatever it is they do, their purpose has to be in relation to the want of the main character.

However, just because they are supporting the journey of the protagonist doesn't mean that they only have a passive role in the story. On the contrary, they are very active characters. Who does the main character turn to, confide in, or even reject as the story progresses? In *The Fighter (2010)* the mother is trying to help her son's career, but she fails. Is she out to sabotage her son, or is she too proud to realize that the responsibilities of being an agent are beyond her?

There needs to be a dynamic energy between the supporting character and all of the other characters in the story. The problem in many screenplays is that the writers want the protagonist to always take the lead. The other characters follow along and fill in the dead space in the story.

Many times, the supporting character has to take up the torch and run with it when the protagonist is feeling weak or vulnerable. Other times, they steal the torch. *A Simple Plan (1998)* had two brothers involved in taking money that wasn't theirs, though they weren't exactly stealing it. The older brother wasn't quite as smart as the younger one. Although he thought he was doing the right thing, he ended up messing up the plans on many occasions.

To give you an idea of the power of these characters, look at some of the people who have won the Academy Award for Best Supporting Actor. Take, for example, Javier Bardem in *No Country for Old Men (2007)* and Gene Hackman for *Unforgiven (1992)*. In both of these cases, they were the antagonists of the story. Al Pacino was nominated Best Supporting Actor for his role in *The Godfather (1972)* along with James Caan and Robert Duvall. It's interesting, because some people consider Al Pacino to be the main character in that film. But, that film was about his father, Don Corleone, played by Marlon Brando. The Best Supporting Actress roles have gone to Tilda Swinton for *Michael Clayton (2007)*, Rachel Weisz in *The Constant Gardener (2005)*, and Dianne Wiest in *Bullets Over Broadway (1994)*.

The supporting characters help us understand who the protagonist is. If you want to get into the mind of the main character, you can explain who or what they are in an on-the-nose manner. But that doesn't make for interesting storytelling, and it won't get your script in the winner's circle. Instead, use the supporting roles to create dialogue or situations with the main character to reveal who they are.

This is all about building relationships, which is what movies are about. Throughout the story we witness the protagonist act and react to the challenges that are posed to them. This is one way for us to understand who they are and what they stand for.

Another way to know them is to watch their relationships unfold with other people in the story. Who do they trust and why? How do they treat other people, how do others treat them? In the film *Night Shift (1982)*, we quickly see how the protagonist goes through life, as a pushover. We wouldn't know all this if it weren't for the supporting characters in his life: his boss, the manic fiancée, the loyal prostitute, or the crazy partner who turns his life around. *The Truman Show (1998)* had an entire community of suburbanites created just to tell the story of Truman's life as a daily soap opera. That's how secondary characters should work in your screenplay, except not as blatant as it was in that film.

Think of your script as a birthday party. Different people with various personalities are getting together for a celebration. Most of the people will get along, but maybe a strange relative will create a few awkward moments. A klutzy friend will spill red wine on the white carpet, somebody will show up late, as usual. However, everything going on is somehow related to the birthday party.

The weird uncle who showed hasn't been seen in years but he came because you're his favorite. The red wine was a gift that was supposed to be opened for a special future occasion, the guy showing up late has brought the ex-girlfriend of the birthday boy to the party. They broke up years ago so it's all ancient history, or is it? There you have it, the setting for a low-budget screenplay. It has a group of people who have a wide array of interesting characteristics and they are compressed into a physically small location for a finite period of time. Light the match and enjoy the fireworks.

You can't afford to waste any pages on an underdeveloped character. Even if they are in the story for a couple of scenes, give them something that will leave a positive impact. Remember the blond guy from *Office Space* (1999): "If things go well I might show her my O-face." He stole the show for the few minutes he was in the movie. This doesn't mean you have to develop a great character for every bank teller, cab driver, or other nondescript background person in your script. Just the secondary characters.

Crafting solid characters, even when they aren't as important as the main character and their antagonist, is the difference between an all around great script, and one that may or may not make the cut. Contest judges notice when you've taken the time to make sure that everybody, including the secondary characters, has a stake in your screenplay.

Sean Hinchey

CASTING

When a judge turns to the first page of your screenplay, they are going to quickly get into the groove about what your story is about. After roughly ten pages, they get familiar with the characters. Now comes some very big questions.

What actor would play the role of the main character? What about the supporting characters? The antagonist? The villain?

Before you even begin writing your next script or perform a rewrite on your current one, make a list of actors who would fill in all of the major roles.

This will help you get a better grip on who your characters are. You may want an older character to have the sly wit of Jack Nicholson or the the smooth grace of Ian Holm. Your younger characters may be from a popular television show or a movie that you recently saw. Try to stay away from coming up with only A-List actors to play your characters. If you see Tom Hanks as playing the role perfectly, see if you can come up with a few other actors who could also work.

This process will help you formulate the quirks your characters have. For example, Adam Sandler has a funny way of speaking softly when he is angry, then his voice slowly gets louder until it's a raspy yell. Tom Wilkinson has a skill for stammering that shows that his character is frazzled, but still in control of the situation. He can be remorseful in one scene, but baring his teeth in the next.

As you write your dialogue, having a short list of actors in your mind will help you create dynamic and realistic exchanges. It's like having a puppet show in your head, where you get to control the actors. You are able to bring the best performances of their greatest films together into one brilliant script: the one you are writing.

A casting list will help you write a script that can be produced. Remember, your goal isn't just to win a screenwriting contest. You want to have a quality script that you can shop to production companies. If your script can't be cast, then it can't be made into a movie. This process allows you to ensure that you have viable script that can be produced.

A few years ago a friend of mine was developing a pitch for a computer system that would allow people to create computer-generated images coupled with real life actors, craft musical scores, and have the ability to edit everything together, all in one machine. The problem at the time was that computers didn't have the processing capabilities to handle these demands. He was aware of this, but he still spent countless hours putting a proposal together. In the end, it was all for nothing. The people who were interested in this project wanted to know when it could be delivered. He explained that because of the technical limitations, he wasn't sure that it could be built.

If it can't be built, it can't be sold. The same goes for casting. If you can't figure out who should, or could, be in your story, then it may not be worth writing. Or, if you are struggling to come up with a viable list of actors, then you may have to restructure your script. Years ago, before the current vampire craze on TV and in the movies, there was a contest submission about a small group of seventy-something year old vampires. They were out for revenge against a group of men that had wiped out all of the other vampires.

Sean Hinchey

As I read this screenplay, I began to think about who could be cast in these roles. There aren't a lot of older actors to choose from who could play the role of a vampire. I couldn't see Morgan Freeman, Michael Caine, Dustin Hoffman, or Jon Voight as a vampire. Jack Nicholson played a devil in *The Witches of Eastwick (1987)*, but that was more of a dark comedy. As I flipped through the script, my mind was caught up in trying to cast the movie. Since nobody came to mind, I couldn't "see" the movie. The script never had a chance to make it as finalist.

Other scripts I've read have had well-developed characters that I could easily apply an actor to. One script had a male and a female role similar to the dynamic of Stanley Tucci and Meryl Streep in *The Devil Wears Prada (2006)*. This isn't to say that was the writer's intent, but it helped me create the world in my mind and it made for an easy read.

Be careful when establishing an age to your characters, though. Keep it broad: female mid-20s, male early-50s. You don't need to be more specific than that.

This may seem like splitting hairs. But when it comes to crafting a quality script, the better you are at helping the judge picture an actor, or at least a type of actor in a role, the better your odds are of winning. It could be something as simple as having two characters in a comedy exchanging witty banter like Owen Wilson and Vince Vaughn in their buddy films. Or have your protagonist and villain be evenly matched like Jeff Bridges and Robert Downey Jr. in *Ironman (2008)*.

This isn't to say that you are expecting a contest judge to make this exact connection. They may read your script and picture the villain as Alan Rickman and the protagonist is Ryan Gosling. Success! You've created a screenplay where the judge can populate the script in their mind with relevant actors.

Writing a cast list is something that you do as an exercise to establish the voice and mannerisms of your characters. It's a personal tool. Under no circumstances should you submit this list of actors with your contest submission. It'll look amateurish and desperate. Write the best script you can with actual actors in mind, and the judges will fill in their own choices.

KEY POINTS

- The protagonist needs to be the focus of every scene, especially if he isn't in a particular scene.

- We don't need to know everything about the main character right away; it's about revealing who he is throughout the first and second acts.

- The main character doesn't always have to be likable; make use of the anti-hero.

- When using the anti-hero, make sure the other characters in the story are worse than your anti-hero.

- Great villains need to be charismatic.

- If your protagonist is smart, the villain needs to be even smarter to be effective.

- If you overlook your secondary characters, the judge will overlook your chances of winning.

- Whatever the secondary character does, it has to be in relation to helping the protagonist get what he wants.

- If you can't think of specific actors to play the roles in your screenplay, then who can?

- A casting list can help you give a certain voice to your characters. But don't submit it with your script.

SIX: GENRES

GENRE & THEME

Before putting down your first words on the page, you have to know what the **theme** is of your script. The theme is the underlying message. The blockbuster film *Avatar* (2009) had a message about saving our planet and the negative aspects of exploiting people and their natural resources for financial gain. In the original *Invasion of the Body Snatchers* (1956), it's been said that the theme had to do with the House Un-American Activities Committee and the requirement that people in the film industry give up the names of others who may have been communists. Every story has a theme, though it doesn't necessarily have to be full of deep thoughts or make a statement about the current political climate. However, it is the moral compass of your story.

How do you go about establishing a proper theme in your story? First, understand why you decided to write the screenplay that you are currently working on. Did you want to tell a story about family dynamics, achieving success when the odds are against the characters, or is it a hero's journey about saving the world?

When you are talking to someone about your script and they ask you, "What are you trying to say?", what they mean is that your theme isn't clear. Like the want of your protagonist, the theme needs to be universal. Figuring out the theme of your script should be easy.

Go back to the inspiration for you script. That is where you derive your theme. Patrick Sheane Duncan was inspired to write *Mr. Holland's Opus* (1995) when he was stuck in traffic because of a school teacher's protest rally. He wanted to write something that would focus on the plight of a teacher, the unsung heroes who sacrifice so much.

In addition to understanding the theme of your script, you need to be clear what genre it falls into. One misconception that writers fall victim to is to not bother with defining their genre so that they won't be "pigeon-holed" to that particular category of screenplay. There is a big distinction between being stuck writing a specific type of film genre and being able to *define* your material. This is very important because the writer who doesn't understand these differences may find himself trying to break into the entertainment industry at a disadvantage.

If an agent, manager, or mentor tells you to stick to a specific genre of screenwriting, that is pigeon-holing you. They are trying to categorize you according to a specific writing style that you have. There are two schools of thought on this.

First, until you actually sell or gain some serious interest in your script or writing skills, you shouldn't anchor yourself to one specific genre. If you feel comfortable switching from drama to comedy, give it a shot. Actors often times go back and forth between different categories. John Lithgow is a perfect example of an incredibly serious drama actor who has played a villain to perfection, yet he shines in comedy. He's won an Emmy Award in each category.

The second line of thinking is that as a writer you want to create a niche for yourself. By mastering a specific style of writing, you can become the main person whom everyone seeks out for your skill set.

Whichever way you feel about these two lines of thought, know that defining your genre in terms of a logline, pitch, or casual conversation is something completely different from being pigeon-holed. When I've consulted with various writers, it still amazes me how many of them are offended when I ask them what genre of script they have written or are thinking about writing next.

As the writer, you have the power. You can write about anything you wish, regardless of what anybody tells you. Agents and managers often specialize in specific genres of films, particularly if they are representing talent that dominates a specific type of filmmaking. You're not going to pitch a World War II film to a manager whose stable of actors are A-Listers in the comedy world. Don't take it personally when people ask about the genre of script you are writing. It's strictly a way to get to know you and the material you are writing. Most important, if you are unclear of what genre of script you are writing for, then your script most likely will lack focus.

What does all of this have to do with writing for a screenplay contest? As we've talked about before, and we will again, you are writing material that will have a life outside the realm of contests. You need to be prepared to present your material to serious people in the film industry. If you are able to understand the pitfalls of writing different genres, you can hone your writing skills to create a solid screenplay worthy of the judge's attention. I can immediately spot a serious writer who understands their craft.

It's like giving a presentation at work. In the first few moments it's very clear who did their homework: the preparation of their visuals, their clear communication skills, the way they take and answer questions, and their energy level. How you prepared doesn't matter; it's all about the execution of your material. The same goes for writing a screenplay. A contest judge won't read your script and think that you've worked hard on developing the structure or took a writing class on dialogue or spent countless hours understanding genres. All they know is either you know have skills or you don't.

With that said, let's delve into the different genres of screenplays that you may have written or are currently working on.

DRAMA

Drama screenplays have always proven to be a solid, marketable genre to write. Most of the A-List actors who are successfully employed have either started in or have mastered the art of working in the genre of drama. A quick internet search of the top actors, either by box office draw or popularity, will get you mostly drama actors. Is this because dramas are easy to write?

Not at all. There isn't any easy genre of screenwriting. The key to writing any great screenplay is to tell a small story well. What makes dramas an easy sell is that life is full of drama. I've often joked that if it weren't for World War II, police officers, and lawyers, there would be only three movies made a year.

There is an enormous amount of material out there that can be mined to write a well-developed and gripping drama. Real life is full of wonderful ideas that are there for the taking. The tag-line for the incredibly successful TV show *Law and Order* is "Ripped from the headlines!"

Flipping through a newspaper or magazine or watching TV news offers a wide array of dramatic material. Life rights are being bought up every day. While only a fraction of them actually get developed into projects, dramas catch people's eyes. It's real life with a twist. Unless you are writing a strict biopic on a person, there are liberties that can be taken with dramas. You can create composite characters. If you have several people in real life who were influential to the story, you can meld them all into one character to create smoother storytelling.

Dramas offer a great opportunity to develop a character. You can really push your protagonists and their nemesis to the breaking point. Torment your protagonist, only to have them succeed in the end. This offers a great challenge as a writer to create enormous obstacles for them, which works if you can successfully get them out of their binds.

However, dramas have to be great-good just isn't good enough. You need to create your script as if your future writing career is riding on it, because it is. If done poorly, you've wasted the contest judge's time and have made no progress. Every scene needs to shine and the dialogue needs to pop off the page while the story moves steadily forward. Because there is so much real life drama to draw upon, some of the heavy lifting is already done for you. There's little excuse for poor execution which will disappoint the judge.

There are many drama scripts written, so you have to put a finer point on what kind of drama you are writing. Is it a police-drama, crime-drama, adventure-drama, epic-drama? Why is it important to define the second tier?

Let's think positively and assume you win a screenwriting contest. When you meet with agents, managers, and actors, they'll want to know more about your script. If you tell them it's a drama, that's not enough detail for them to understand what you are presenting to them. If your award-winning script is an action-drama, for example, you are helping them visualize what your script is about before you even pitch it to them.

Today's entertainment market is very fragmented. Not so long ago, entertainment was basically limited to television, movies, and theater. Today, you can play videogames with graphics so incredible it's like directing a movie in real time. There's web-based content you can watch on your computer or smart phone. These minimovies are bite-sized stories that you can watch at your leisure. Cable TV networks generate their own content, and movies often go straight to DVD.

Defining the drama one step further helps you craft a better quality screenplay. It takes it out of the realm of everyday drama and sets it in the context of a more refined niche. Not only will it make it easier for a contest judge to understand what your script is about, it'll also allow you to focus on the writing process. In the end, that'll get you one step closer to a winning screenplay.

Sean Hinchey

COMEDY

There's an old saying: "Dying is easy, comedy is hard." This is a truth that cannot be realized until one actually attempts to write a comedy. The majority of comedy scripts that I have read are lacking in one simple department. They just aren't **funny**. However, this is only half of the equation. Comedies can't only be funny; they also have to be **smart**. The problem is, too many people who attempt to write comedies are trying very hard to be **clever.**

In order to understand how to write a comedy, you must understand what we mean when we're discussing **funny, smart, and clever.** So that we can reach that point, we are going to talk about a few specific comedies. If you haven't seen them, and you are attempting to write, or think you have written, a comedy, you will need to watch these films more than once.

When Harry Met Sally (1989) isn't just a comedy, it is a Romantic-Comedy or Rom-Com. These can be some of the most difficult types of comedies to write because they have to touch on the sensitive matter of relationships in a humorous but respectful manner. The reason why this movie works is because this movie is very **funny**. What do we mean by funny? We want the judge to laugh. While this may sound easy to do, it isn't.

A writer can make someone laugh by using physical humor. There are pratfalls, a runaway car chasing down a group of nuns or bodily function noises, as just a few examples. This physical type of humor plays more on the visual aspect of comedy. Granted, this can make for some very funny moments. Unfortunately too many scripts throw one physical moment in after another. There needs to be witty exchanges and good-natured verbal sparring. The writer usually doesn't spend enough time writing solid dialogue in the majority of comedy contest entries.

When Harry Met Sally has some incredible exchanges. It revolves around the differences between men and women, while being witty, insightful yet respectful. The story doesn't need to rely on physical comedy, though there is one great physical comedy scene that takes place in a restaurant. Recognize that while a writer may be attempting to put a funny scene on paper, that description may not come across as clearly to a contest judge as it does to the writer.

However, funny dialogue will capture a judge's attention every time. The writer of *When Harry Met Sally*, Nora Ephron, crafted the dialogue in such a carefully, well-constructed manner that it not only gets the point across, it gives permission for the audience to laugh at some awkward situations.

What about the scripts that aren't Romantic-Comedies? *Dirty Rotten Scoundrels (1988)* is a well-written story. Since the script deals with con artists, the script has to be ruthless but in a funny manner. The title perfectly summarizes the two main characters as they try to outdo each other. However, there's nothing overly mean or sinister about either one of them. While they are criminals, they aren't the violent type. We know that they will only be after their victim's money, but they won't resort to murder. The tone of this film is established early on.

What makes them likable is that they are going after wealthy people. This doesn't excuse their crime, but since they are going after small amounts of cash in relation to what their quarry can afford to lose, we allow it. Had the story been written where they were taking advantage of people living in poverty, then they would be ugly and despicable to us.

This makes for *smart* writing. While having well-developed characters is important, the contest judge has to like who they are as a person. Writers often times try to make the character sarcastic or a bit brusque. While this can add an edge to that personality, when it goes too far the judge will feel alienated from the character.

This is the difference between writing *smart* or just trying to be *clever*. Comedy scripts submitted into contests try to populate the dialogue with snappy banter. While it may be cleverly barbed or full of innuendo, if the story isn't propelled forward then the comedy will be lost in the noise. Having a mean or jaded quality will not make for an interesting character. The exception to the rule is if the comedy is about a curmudgeon changing his or her ways by the end of the movie. This was the character arc in As Good As It Gets (1997). Had that main character been used in a context where he was unwilling or unable to change, the negative aspects about his character may have dragged down the entire script.

Comedy writing is about humor, but the other aspects that deal with dialogue, character exposition, and storytelling hold true in this genre. Another common problem with comedies in contest scripts is that the writer sacrifices structure, hoping that the humor and tone of the story will win over a contest judge. The three act structure applies to all genres of screenplays.

Comedies still have conflict-it's just that the conflict is told in a lighter tone than in other genres. A large number of scripts try to be funny, or even just clever, right out of the gate. But, what the main character wants is never made clear. Without a clear goal for the protagonist to go after, there is no way for the judge to tune into the story.

Never let the concept or physical comedy overshadow the basic elements that create excellent story telling. There are no shortcuts. Simply being funny isn't enough to make for a contest-winning comedy script.

Sean Hinchey

SCIENCE FICTION (SCI-FI)

Science Fiction is a very difficult genre to master at a level that would win a screenwriting contest.

First, science fiction movies are very *expansive* to make. That is correct, expansive, not expensive. There are new worlds that are imagined, various exotic creatures and technologies beyond that which exists now. Part of being a good judge is the ability to imagine the script as a movie on a big screen. Your job as a writer is to successfully craft the world for the judge to visualize. The majority of the time, writers fail at properly developing this complex world.

If you are creating new machines and technologies or a planet with unusual ecosystems, you need to be brief and to the point. Obviously, the whole point of writing science fiction is to create a new world or an entire universe. However, if your script is reading like an encyclopedia filled with facts, then you will need to retool your material. The universe that you are creating isn't what the story is about. It's only the setting.

The more complex you make the story, the harder a judge has to work to get their mind around it. It's very easy for a contest judge to tune out because the writer has gotten in way over their head. How do you prove that your script is worthy of becoming a contest-winning script? When describing something that hasn't been seen before in real life, make sure that it is relevant to the story.

Many scripts have in-depth descriptions about the drive system of an enormous spaceship, for example. Another story had detailed a futuristic computer system that the writer crafted like an owner's manual. The problem with these scripts was that none of the material revealed has any relevance to the story.

If you have a flying machine that our protagonist uses, it doesn't matter if it runs on a crystal-hyperdrive system with random interval spacing. I'm not sure that even makes sense, but it's similar to the made up technological terms used in many sci-fi scripts. In the movie *Dune (1984)* there was an enormous amount of detail about a mineral used to transport oneself instantaneously through space. The reason: the entire story was about different kingdoms trying to take control of this rare substance.

Keep the technological babble to a minimum unless it is relevant to the main goal of the protagonist. In *Total Recall (1990)* we learned about the ancient Martians because the payoff was about the humans activating an alien device that could change the entire eco-system of Mars. The writer was careful to only introduce us to the technology as it related to the main character's journey. The rest is left to our imagination. In *Star Wars (1977)* we know that a light saber will cut off a person's limbs, but we never delve into the technology that makes it possible, because it doesn't matter. However, it is vital to know that a port-hole not much bigger than a womp-rat is the weak link in the Death Star.

Another reason that many science fiction stories fail to advance in screenwriting contests is that they don't have a universal theme. Many a sci-fi script has tried to get too clever with the mythology that's been created, but the story suffers. The overall background of a sci-fi script won't replace poorly executed storytelling.

For example, *Blade Runner (1982)* is a detective story

set in the future. It has the same film noir feel as *Double Indemnity (1944)* with the good hooks of the Humphrey Bogart films. The protagonist is chasing down a group of criminals, but the sci-fi twist is that they are synthetic, artificially created life forms. The "Matrix" trilogy movies are Kung-Fu films, the "Star Wars" franchise is based around the Akira Kurosawa samurai films. *Outland (1981)* is *High Noon (1952)* in space, and *Avatar (2009)* is a CGI version of *Dances with Wolves (1990)*. The list goes on and on.

On the other hand, films such as *Battlefield Earth (2000)* is lacking in any interesting backstory or universal theme. The film was too caught up in the visual effects and tried to have slick costumes and clever dialogue. There just wasn't much of a story present. In the end, you can't carve rotted wood. Some of the "Star Trek" movies have fizzled. The writers relied too much on the "cool factor" surrounding the franchise.

Think of a science fiction film as a different backdrop for a theme that can be utilized in other genres. At the core of your story, there needs to be a quest that everyone reading your script can understand, or even better, relate to. Chances are, the science fiction films that you may have seen and didn't like were lacking in this universal connection. But someone like Luke Skywalker in *Star Wars* had a quest that everyone could relate to. He was a simple farmer who wanted to leave it all behind to join the rebellion in their journey to defeat the evil empire. It's that universal feeling of wanting to start over and save the world.

In the end, all scripts are about storytelling. Focus on crafting a great backstory and keep it simple. Don't fall into the trap of having the world you've created be the strongest part of your screenplay. Anyone can create a new world. Only the best writers can fill it with a solid narrative.

Sean Hinchey

HORROR

When a horror movie strikes gold, Hollywood flushes the bushes looking for the next horror flick to bring to the big screen.

Horror scripts have an advantage over other genres, but there are also several disadvantages. Several contests only accept horror films for their entries. Coupled with the fact that there aren't many other genre-specific contests, this allows writers who have a completed horror script to get a leg up on other writers. If you are an avid horror writer, you may submit more than one of your screenplays, and you won't have to compete with other genres of scripts. The odds are in your favor of winning this type of contest.

Before you get too excited, though, beware of the downfalls to writing a horror movie.

Most contest judges don't like reading horror movies. This has nothing to do with them not liking the genre itself. Most of the horror movies that are submitted to contests (not the horror-only contests) are poorly written and rely on too much gore. We will talk about this aspect later.

The writer has to overcome the preconceived notion of what a solid horror script should be like. How do you go about doing that? Write a solid story. This may sound trite, but really work on crafting great characters in a well-developed setting. However, as with sci-fi, don't let the setting overcome the theme of your script.

The majority of horror scripts that I've read for contests spend an enormous amount of time elaborating on the scenes. Be it a dungeon, abandoned warehouse, or some type of haunted house. Use that location as a backdrop. Don't fall so in love with the setting that you sacrifice every other aspect of your script. But, here's the tricky part. Many times, the location is a character in the story. For example, assume your script has a building where somebody was murdered and now the building has taken on an evil personality. You would need to develop that building just as you would a human character.

That building needs to have flaws, strengths and weaknesses. The evil that has inhabited that structure has given it human-like attributes. This goes beyond creaking floors or chipped paint. What does that structure want? Maybe it wants everyone to die, or suffer an eternity of fear. When developing an inanimate object as a character, it's about crafting personality.

The Shining (1980) takes place in a large hotel tucked in the mountains. The description of the sheer size and the isolation it offers is important because the hotel becomes a character. The Bates Motel in *Psycho (1960)* still maintains a clean façade with its working neon lights. This is a little strange considering that nobody travels that road anymore. The prison hospital in *The Silence of the Lambs (1991)* has personality because it relates to the quirks of the villain. In all of these cases, the description in the screenplay was just enough to shape these locations as characters. There wasn't anything extraneous to illustrate these areas like one would when writing a novel.

The film *Event Horizon (1997)* is a sci-fi, horror movie. The writer did a phenomenal job of giving the spaceship personality. It had desires, strengths, and weaknesses just like a person. These quirks had to be layered in gradually so that we accepted the ship as more than just an inanimate vessel with people trapped inside. The ship was responsible for imprisoning them. The same goes for HAL in *2001: A Space Odyssey* (1968), the computer had human characteristics. Not only did it sound like a person, but it was paranoid, a trait one wouldn't expect from a computer.

Therefore, if you are writing a story and the building is just a benign structure where the horrors take place, then go easy on the descriptions. Don't talk about the creaky floorboards unless that ties directly into the story. If you talk about the chipped paint, then maybe the paint was brand new in an early scene. This decay could stand for something specific in the story. By delving into the storytelling and crafting solid and meaningful dialogue between the terrified inhabitants, you will create a memorable script that will captivate the judge's attention. The exchanges need to be more than them saying they are scared. Maybe they admit to past transgressions to clear their soul before they die.

Another problem with horror movies occurs when the writer doesn't craft an exciting and gripping story. The writer relies on hackneyed scare scenes or strange characters that are meant to grab the judge's attention. These ploys rarely work. While it is acceptable to have them in your script, you shouldn't expect these aspects to do all the heavy lifting.

It's amazing how many horror scripts still have teens wandering off into an abandoned amusement park or splitting up to investigate strange sounds. These scenes have been done so many times that they've even been parodied in pop culture. What makes for an effective horror movie is when someone wanders into a normal situation that becomes something tragic.

For example, *Poltergeist (1982)* is about a family whose home is invaded by evil spirits. By the end of the film, we realize that an entire home development was built upon an old graveyard. The spirits of the disturbed bodies have taken out their revenge on the residents. What makes this story work so well is that the people are working- and middle-class families with kids in school and day jobs. They aren't looking for trouble; instead the trouble has come to them. The horror has entered their very home. What could be more personal and frightening than that? If it could happen to them, then it could happen to you!

This isn't to say that every horror movie has to be in the main character's home or office. Many of the scripts have situations where it's clear that the main character, or characters, are going to get into a weird and horrific situation. For example, one contest submission had a group of teens try to track down a reclusive horror writer on his secluded island. The entire place was rigged with danger. The problem was that the setup was so blatant that it didn't work. It tried too hard to be a horror movie. What might have saved this script is if each of the dangers was based on something in one of the author's previous books. If the final trap had been something from an unreleased novel, that could be a good hook. Never write the screenplay that says, "I'm a horror-script." The best written ones start off with the main characters on a normal day. As the the judge flips the pages, they slowly descend into a different world and the adventure begins.

A problem with many horror scripts is that they can be too gory. Sometimes known as "horror-porn," these stories have a great deal of blood and guts in them. This is unfortunate because when the movie going public hears the term "horror movie," they no longer associate it with a good scare. The special effects of blood and body parts leap to mind instead.

The same goes for many contest judges. As soon as they open the first page, they may already wincing. The expectation is that it'll be gross with no redeeming qualities. How do you overcome this? Make it clear in the early pages that your story will not be a gore-fest. While a well-placed scene here and there to shock the judge is acceptable, if you start off with a person suffering a grotesque fate, you may have lost your chance at winning.

It's about creating tension and suspense. In the film *Jaws (1975)*, which is a horror movie that takes place on the water, there are a few shots showing some severed limbs. However, they are very brief and it's that moment of brevity that adds to the entire shock value of the movie. Even the fate of Quint, who spits up blood as the shark bites down on him, is relevant because of his obsession with catching the great white shark. The opening scene with the woman attacked by the shark is shot very tight at water level, no blood but great tension. The mayhem is in the theater of the mind.

Keep any gore and blood proportional to the story. It's always better to show less and allow the audience to imagine more in their story. *Marathon Man (1976)* has a dentist who drills into the protagonist's tooth to try to get him to give up information. We hear the whirling of the drill as the camera slowly pans away. The scene is much more effective because of this technique. Show less, and let the audience imagine more. Alfred Hitchcock was a genius at allowing the audience to complete the scene in their mind.

As with every genre of screenplay, the script works best

when the focus is on the story. Instead of resorting to shock value, capture the contest judge's attention with well-developed characters. Allow them to warm up to the story by slowly setting up the scenario of what will befall the main characters. Create a solid villain so that by the time you lead the judge into the main crux of your script, they will be ready for anything you throw at them.

Sean Hinchey

PERIOD PIECE

Everybody has an idea for a period piece, one that captures the rich, nostalgic background of a specific era. However, there are a few major issues that need to be overcome when crafting any period piece. By period piece we are talking about Ancient Rome or Greece, the Victorian Era, Civil War, World War II, or any time, really, before the present day.

The first major problem that any period piece runs into is the cost. Remember, you are writing a script that will not only try to capture the top prize in a screenwriting contest but will also be a viable product to shop at different production companies. There are very few companies that have the financial resources to create a period piece. Costumes, locations, vehicles, and other specific considerations unique to this genre ratchet up the costs. It's something to consider. You may win a contest, but you'll generate little interest in your script.

The overall cost of what a screenplay would be-in actual dollars and cents-isn't what will sink or save your screenplay from advancing to the finalist round or even winning the contest. What can hurt you is if you haven't adequately captured the essence of that period without getting too involved in the era as the main focus.

The majority of period piece scripts that I've come across are laden with heavy description regarding the costumes or customs of that specific era. While this is vital to give the flavor of that time, it's clear that the writer has fallen in love with the era they are writing about, at the cost of the story. While heavy description works well for a novel, too much of it bogs down anyone reading your script.

Ask yourself, is every detail of a woman's dress or particular chateau vital to the storytelling? In most cases, the writer simply lays down too much information. As a writer, you may have selected a specific color of the main character's cloak. If it isn't germane to the story, don't write about it. While researching that era to get the details right, don't lose yourself in it. The reality is, if your script were to be made into a movie, the red dress you envisioned may end up being blue.

These details will not propel your story forward. When the description gets too dense, a contest judge will switch off and their interest in the script will wane. As an example, one script had almost two full pages describing a ballroom, along with the dishware and tapestries where a scene was taking place.

None of these finer details had any importance to the story. The scene fell flat. What was assumed to be a buildup to a vital twist in the script ended up being nothing more than opulent pageantry. There was dancing and idle gossip throughout the scene, but the story wasn't propelled forward by these details, and the characters weren't especially interesting.

Imagine your period piece characters in a basic white room, wearing sweat pants and a T-Shirt. Would their stories, dialogue, and character development be compelling as you've written them?

Ask yourself, does your script have to take place in this era? If your characters fall flat in the stark setting that I've posed in the previous paragraph, then they probably won't work in a more embellished environment of the period piece. If there isn't a story, then all the detailed descriptions won't cover up for its hollow core.

Sean Hinchey

Make sure your story is intact, that it flows logically and can express its universal theme to the judge. For example, *Marie Antoinette (2006)* is about a young, naive woman who indulges in a life of luxury while the peasants in France are in poverty. However, this life of excess could also be told in contemporary times. The background could during the dot-com bust of the late 1990s. The main character could be the wife of a power player who is pilfering the wealth of his company while the stock prices drop. The story could be set against the recent real estate bust that has created a worldwide recession. It's all about having a story that can become culturally relevant, regardless of what the background is. That's why ancient mythology still works to this day. The gods have the flaws and characteristics that humans have. Their stories are about lust, greed, envy, ambition, and narcissism.

Last Man Standing (1996) is a remake of *Yojimbo (1961)*, a story set in the 19th century. The new version works because it has a solid, universal theme that can be set in different eras. The same idea could be utilized against the setting of a massive space station orbiting a distant planet. In an earlier chapter we talked about *Outland (1981)* being a futuristic remake of *High Noon (1952)*.

Love Affair (1939) is a story about two lovers who agree to put their lives in order before they meet again in six months so they can build a life together. The movie was remade as *An Affair to Remember (1957)* and under the original title again in 1994. Although the core of the story is the same, each one was told in the current era that it was filmed.

Be careful with the dialogue. One contest submission took place during the post-Civil War era in the South.

Some of the retorts by the main characters were, "You're kidding, right?" and "That's not gonna happen!" It just didn't sound like how people would've talked back then. Creating dialogue that captures the cadence, words, and tone of how people spoke in a particular time can be daunting.

When crafting a period piece, there is nothing more important than building the story up from the bottom. That is, have all the vital elements that we've been discussing—structure, dialogue, and character arc—contained in your story. Populate it with specific, relevant details about the era you are writing about. However, never get so caught up in the specifics that the story falters.

It's better to have a well-developed story against a background that may be slightly inaccurate historically than an overdeveloped tapestry without substance. The judge will always choose story over spectacle.

Sean Hinchey

WESTERNS

Just like period pieces, Westerns can be a tough sell because of the cost of making them. In addition to expensive sets, there are almost always horses involved, not to mention extensive stunts and expensive location shoots. While interiors can be shot on a sound stage, in today's high-definition world it's hard to substitute exterior shots with anything else but the real McCoy. As with period pieces, you may win the contest, but not be able to sell your script.

What are Western movies about? If you ask the average moviegoer, they are about gun fights, riding into sunsets, stolen loot and often times, tough women. But that's all window dressing. Just like period pieces, it's vital to get away from the grandeur of what a Western looks like and understand what this genre is actually about. There is one common theme that virtually every Western has.

Mostly, they are stories about revenge. An action happens that wrongs another person, and that victim is bent on vengeance. This is very important. While there can be other aspects of the story, at the very least, Westerns are about setting things right.

Granted, there are Westerns that revolve around starting life anew on the frontier. *Little Big Man (1970)* and *Dances with Wolves (1990)* are two examples. However, the conflict still manifests itself to the point where the protagonist has to set things right. This conflict comes about because the person is caught between two worlds: the one they came from and are trying to leave behind, and the new world that they desperately try to become part of. This theme was used in *Avatar (2009)*, which as I mentioned, is a sci-fi *Dances with Wolves*.

Westerns can be detective stories as well. The quarry is tracked, people are shaken down for information, and there are deals and double-crosses. However, all of these actions are to help the main character exact revenge for the wrongs against them and set thing right. In this context, the film *Payback* (1999) is actually a Western. A man is double crossed and left for dead. Now it's time for, as the title says, "Payback." There are shady characters, a damsel in distress, and plenty of gunplay. The entire film could've been shot against the backdrop of a lawless town in the Wild West.

Unforgiven (1992) has detective elements to it. In order to get reward money, the main character has to find a group of cowboys that somebody wants dead. Just as *Payback* could be a Western, *Unforgiven* could be a present day movie.

With Western scripts, most people don't know how to write a proper protagonist or anti-hero. In many of the old Westerns, we have a naive man who has to overcome incredible obstacles to get revenge. In the process, they become something different: a person bordering on evil. This is what makes the Western interesting. It's not about crowding the pages of the screenplay with gun play; it's about the gradual transformation of this individual. There is something likable about them, but we cringe because they have to do the unspeakable to set things right. By the end of the story we either like them more, or maybe we lose some respect for them.

The main character in *Unforgiven* has a sordid past that we become familiar with. Despite all of his attempts to maintain himself as an honest citizen, and a changed man, he is drawn back into darkness. Early on we see him as a farmer who is barely getting by. Killing for money is all that he knows. *The Man Who Shot Liberty Valance (1962)* features a lawyer who is trying to bring order to a Western town. At one point, he has to put down his books and take up a gun. Sometimes you need to enforce the ink on the page with lead from a bullet. Hey, that's pretty deep, if I do say so myself.

It's this transformation that keeps a contest judge riveted to the page. It could be from good to bad, or bad to good back to bad. While a gunfight, horse chase, and a train heist are all interesting and fun things to write, they've been done before in many different combinations. Great Westerns are about the characters and usually they are anti-heroes or reluctant heroes.

Utilizing the technology, or lack of it, is one way to maximize the background of the Wild West. If a man arrives to clean up a dusty, old town there are no cell phones for the sheriff to use. The roads may not be well marked, so making a fast getaway is impossible or difficult. Everything unfolds on a smaller and often times, slower pace. However, if *Unforgiven* were told in a modern setting, the cowboys in danger might've put up security cameras outside their cabin. They would've been in greater contact with the sheriff.

Explore the limitations that the Western genre has to offer. That is meant in the positive sense. Play on the lack of education the people have, the fact that mail takes weeks to be delivered or that the only place to get information is the saloon which could be owned by the protagonist or villain. In the process of writing, never lose perspective of what the main core of the story is. If you have one shootout after another, with no room for the main character to grow or transform, then you have no story.

Keep the goals of the main characters simple and never let them stray off their path. The world of the Western should enhance the story, not hide any flaws in your premise.

Sean Hinchey

THRILLER

A truly well written Thriller, especially a Psychological-Thriller, will have most contest judges push your script right to the top of the pile. No matter how many times this subject matter has been tackled, there are always new and fresh ways to make it relevant. Most fans of this genre may find themselves flipping through TV channels and getting sucked into a Hitchcock film, even if it has already started. There's something so wonderful about the twists and turns that makes one want to see the same thriller again and again.

There are several major problems with writing a thriller. If these pitfalls can be avoided, and you have a solid concept, you could be on your way to winning the next contest.

Many writers fail to have a firm grasp of the subject matter. The reason why these stories are so popular is that a good writer makes the story look so easy to craft. Before embarking on the journey of writing a thriller, map out your script. There have been many scripts where I've been eagerly flipping the pages in anticipation of a great payoff. The writer, more often than not, paints herself into a corner and the character's method of getting unstuck is implausible or just unrealistic. There is a specific example of this in the film *Ronin* (1998).

At one point, the two main characters lose track of their quarry and find themselves on the run, but they are able to hole up at a friend's home. When one of the main characters talks to his old friend, he makes it clear that the trail has gone cold. The master of the house responds somberly that he will find the man they are looking for. In the next scene, the two main characters are hot on the trail of their prey. This causes a huge problem that has been evident in many screenplays entered into script contests. How did the characters get back into the game with just one phone call?

A writer can put the characters into as much jeopardy as they want. One of the best parts about reading a psychological thriller is seeing how far the writer can push the protagonist before they bounce back. Most writers fail when it comes to restoring their main character on the path to getting what they want.

In Greek and Roman drama, there is a term called *deus ex machina*, which means divine intervention. In many of the theater pieces, a person dressed as one of the gods would swoop down like Spider-Man and rescue a person from distress. Other times, they may just appear on stage from the side or through a trap door and save the day. This device required little imagination on the part of the writer. The audiences in those days probably weren't quite as discriminating or critical as they are today—and their gods were busy interfering with mortal lives all the time.

Never have any device in your script where your characters suddenly get out of a tight situation by some previously unnamed or unaddressed resource. One of the great elements of a thriller is that even the smallest detail about a character may come into play so they can get out of a bind. It could be a piece of information, a special skill, or a physical item they have on them.

The Manchurian Candidate (1962) had a soldier who has been brainwashed. He was programmed to be susceptible to suggestions whenever he saw the Queen of Diamonds playing card. In a twist later in the story, his fiancée shows up at a costume party dressed as a Queen of Diamonds card, which temporarily throws events into a spiral. It is the use of significant details such as these that make for a tense thriller.

Another problem that needs to be overcome when writing a solid thriller is having a great payoff that is proportional to the story. In North by Northwest (1959), the main character is caught up in a case of mistaken identity and is on the run for his life. However, there aren't any gun fights in the story, so our protagonist isn't armed. However, he does have to outsmart his enemy, even though he isn't sure who they are. It wouldn't be proportional for the main character to run around shooting the bad guys.

Fargo (1996) has some very unsavory people in it. If you aren't sufficiently armed, then you may not make it out alive. What makes this movie work is that you have a pregnant protagonist who sees some horrific things in her job, while she goes home every night to a loving husband as they prepare to bring a new life into the world. There is a great deal of tension, but also a lot of tenderness set against a stark background.

In The Sum of All Fears (2002), the protagonist is almost killed when his helicopter is knocked out of the sky by a nuclear blast. His near death is proportional to the events happening around him. If a detective is investigating a serial murderer, then their life also needs to be on the line. In Tightrope (1984), the protagonist almost loses his life while investigating a serial murderer, and his family ends up paying a heavy price.

Jaws (1975) turns into a life or death battle against an eating machine. When the captain is killed before the protagonist's eyes and his friend is presumed dead, a sheriff who is afraid of the water has to fight to the finish. *Se7en (1995)* had two detectives hunting an unknown criminal who was killing people according to the seven deadly sins. Once they got on his trail, their own lives were in jeopardy. For the detectives to find their prey, they need to get into his mind, which is a very ugly place.

Successful thrillers establish early on what is at stake for the protagonist. Is it the safety of our president or a weapon about to fall into enemy hands? Is it a case of mistaken identity or a murder for hire that doesn't make sense?

In all of these examples, the story is somewhat simple. They are very easy to pitch and they flow logically. There's a tendency to put in layer upon layer, or twist after twist into a thriller. While it is important to have a few "gotcha" moments where things aren't what they seem, the scripts that have too many turns of the screw are usually lacking a cohesive story.

A good thriller is about keeping the audience engaged in the story through the arc of the main characters. How can one know what the protagonist is capable of if we never glean who they are as a person? What are their strengths and weaknesses, their fears or accomplishments? A good twist without solid characters does not make for a great screenplay.

One contest submission had a good setup. A heist was being planned by a group of small time crooks on an art gallery. Instead of going after the art, they were going after something less tangible, yet far more lucrative. There was information in the safe that could be used to blackmail a wealthy individual.

Sean Hinchey

The script presented a nice twist on a heist theme, along the lines of *Inside Man* (2006). The main problem had to do with the underdeveloped characters. There was a budding romance between the leader of the group and an ex-girlfriend who lived in the town where the heist takes place. By the end of the story, the couple are heading out of town together. There was no chemistry between them, no slow buildup, and no established history regarding their past. Why did they break up in the first place?

The writer spent no time establishing the relationships between the men in the group. Were they old friends? Did they all get along or was there friction between a few of them? All of them came across like faceless mannequins in the story. The description about how the heist would unfold was too dense. Many scenes were devoted to them planning the date of the crime, what tools they would use and how they would escape without getting caught. Yet, there was nothing substantial happening. It was a plot in search of a story.

Usually the case with many writers is that they fall in love with the story and that's what they focus their energies on developing. When somebody leaves a movie theater, the plot is what they think they are talking about. What audiences don't realize is that it's really the characters that they liked. It's how the characters are developed that pushes the story forward and moves the plot along.

Never sacrifice solid storytelling by only developing the concept or plot. Always remember that without great, three dimensional characters, even the best idea will fall flat. If the concept is the vehicle, the characters are the fuel that keeps it moving.

FAMILY

Family movies will always have a solid place in the world of filmmaking. There are excellent themes that can be explored and lessons to be taught. A common theme is: believe in yourself.

Most family scripts fail through a common pitfall that can be overcome with a little bit of work. They try to be too cute. While the cuteness factor does come into play in the story, it should never be the payoff.

The best way to write a family-based script is to work it backwards. What is the **one** message you are trying to get across? This is very important, and it's vital to focus on the specific word, one. Family stories will not work if there are too many messages that are trying to be portrayed. The script will be disjointed and may come across as preachy.

For example, let's say that there is a high school student who comes from a broken home and is trying to get into college. What does college represent in the context of this story? It could be a better life, job opportunities, independence, or a major change in the character's current situation. Everything in the story needs to be solely about that person making the right choices so that this dream becomes a reality. What happens is that most writers lose the story by trying to solve too many other problems.

You can't have the student work hard at getting the parents back together and reconciling. There is an exception to this. If, somehow, reuniting the parents helps the student get into college, then the story can focus on this aspect. Maybe the parents are living in separate homes, if they reunite they'll live under one roof and the money they'll be saving could pay for college.

However, if the story turns into the student trying to fix everything before they leave for college, the story will falter. There are going to be other relevant obstacles that the main character will have to deal with. However, it only works if the end outcome is in relation to them getting into college.

For example, the protagonist should not be trying to put down the high school bully, get a date to the prom, or be the most popular person in the school. Like the above example, all of this can be worked into the story only if it ties into the main goal of the character. Many writers put too much extraneous information into the story because they believe it enriches the world they've created. In reality they've muddled the story with many scenes that have little to do with the character's goal.

What we would want to see is hard choices that would affect the goal of going to college: sacrifice. Instead of going to a house party, the protagonist works at a soup kitchen so they can have some volunteering time on their college application. There may be tough choices regarding a boyfriend or girlfriend. A date has to be broken because the SAT is the next day.

Sacrifice is a very important aspect that is often overlooked. Family movies are about decisions, some of them good, some bad. Either way, we are watching the character grow as they go about their daily routines. That is why the main theme in a family movie is about both growth and sacrifice. What does the main character want? What are they willing to do to get what they want?

Often, this theme gets lost by having scenes showing the different cliques at school. As a contest judge, I've seen this type of writing many times before. It's not mandatory to put these different groups into the story just to fill space. Again, if it helps or hinders the main character on their journey, then use it.

The above examples are used to illustrate just one type of Family movie. No matter what kind of Family script you are writing, keep the theme very simple and universal. One element that family scripts all have in common is that they are about a young person about to make a dramatic life change that everyone can understand.

By young, this doesn't necessarily mean young in age. It also applies to young at heart. A perfect example of this is the Disney-Pixar movie *Up (2009)*. An older man who is now a widow wants to live the dream that he and his wife had always held dear in their hearts.

This is where the concept of second chances comes into play. Despite the age of any character, the goal that they are about to undertake will be one of the biggest challenges of their lives. It's their desire to reach this goal, in relation to where they are at the beginning of the story that makes the script interesting.

Make every scene about one focused goal with a clear theme. Resist the temptation to fill the script with scenes that take away from that journey, especially if you put them in there because "you're supposed to." In the end, you will have a quality story that will capture the heart of any contest judge.

Sean Hinchey

NON-LINEAR

Non-Linear timeline scripts aren't quite their own genre. Nobody would qualify a script simply as a "Non-Linear" story. These are components of storytelling. It could be a Drama or Thriller told in a non-linear way. For the purposes of this chapter, we will treat it like a separate genre of screenwriting.

Why even bring up this method of writing, then? While it wasn't the first screenplay to use this story telling mechanism, *Pulp Fiction (1994)* changed how many people viewed the art of storytelling. Unfortunately it encouraged many writers to mimic this structure, often with disastrous results.

Because of the success of this film, and many other films by Quentin Tarantino, writers assumed that by taking a story, chopping it up, and reassembling the pieces in a mixed up order they would have a seven-figure screenplay to show. This misconception has wasted the time of many writers. Taking a story idea that flows A-B-C-D-E-F-G may work out well. However, if you change that story flow to C-F-B-D-E-G-A it doesn't necessarily work out effectively.

Non-Linear storylines are used to create tension in the story by revealing elements that are out of order. There is a purpose behind it. The story is still cohesively connected. Almost all scripts that I've read using this method have fallen short of their goal. Why do they fail?

Before we answer that question, let's look at a few other films that use this method of storytelling. We're going back in time to *Citizen Kane (1941)*. While this film has understandably landed on multiple Top Ten movie lists, it is a very complex method of storytelling. We see the main character, who is an anti-hero, taking his last gasp and muttering a word that haunts a reporter for the rest of the film, "Rosebud." The story is told in a series of flashbacks as the reporter tries to solve the mystery.

Peeling back the layers, we see a powerful man through different stages of his life. By the end of the film, the audience understands the significance of "Rosebud," but the reporter doesn't. However, it really doesn't matter because both parties have a full understanding of who this man was. This story may not have worked had it been told in chronological order because the suspense wouldn't have been heightened. Telling the story in a non-linear fashion isn't as simple as cutting up a linear story and rearranging the pieces. When transitioning between present and past, there needs to be a hand-off between the scenes. If that connection isn't there, the whole story reads like a series of disjointed scenes.

Mystery Train (1989) tells three different stories, but they are all connected by a gunshot. That point in the story becomes the touchstone which links everything together. Although the story wasn't fantastic, the structure was well thought out. Years ago while working in the story department at International Creative Management (ICM), I read the script for *11:14 (2003)*, which later made it to the screen. Five stories are interconnected because they all touch upon 11:14 at night somewhere within their vignette.

The original screenplay had some flaws with the story, but overall the flow worked. It was easy to turn the pages because I wanted to see how all of these stories would connect to that specific time. The film itself had worked out some of the kinks that were in the script, and it made for a satisfying film.

Sean Hinchey

Writers generally don't have any touchstones that we talked about in the previous examples. The structure of the story is simply a set of bones. Without the connective tissues and muscle, they just lay there in a heap. Especially in non-linear scripts, it's vital to have something consistent in the story to keep everything synchronized. Regardless of what that mechanism is, the protagonist's want has to be scattered throughout the script. It needs to be evident in every scene. Most submissions simply have scenes that never adequately address the goal of the entire story.

Most writers never make it clear why their script needs to use this non-linear method. For example, I'm not sure that *Vanilla Sky (2001)* needed to use be told this way. At times the story was confusing, and the final payoff wasn't worthy of the broken timeline format. There needs to be something about how the ending of the story will be revealed, or a different aspect regarding a character that drives the writer to use this format. A contest judge should be able to finish the script and understand that there was no other way to tell the story. Would *Memento (2000)* work in a traditional format?

Most likely not. The story is about a man trying to remember his past. We go on the journey with him as he tries to piece his life back together. What makes that script interesting is that while we are going back in time, the story is also moving forward into the future. The non-linear timeline works because the flow of the storytelling mimics the protagonist's thought processes.

If you are crafting a screenplay in which you tamper with a chronological timeline, you need to ask yourself: how does this method of storytelling maximize the use of this mechanism?

Many contest-submitted non-linear scripts offer little to no tension in the story. If there isn't going to be a great pay out, an incredible revelation or a twist in the story that nobody would see coming, then why not tell the story chronologically. Here are but a few non-linear films that have powerful endings or messages: *Watchmen (2009), Into the Wild (2007), The Constant Gardener (2005), The Sixth Sense (1999),* and *Rashomon (1950).*

All of these films mined the benefits of telling a story that transports the viewer back and forth through time. The purpose of this is to create tension for a large payoff. *The Constant Gardener* consistently confuses the viewer. Is the protagonist's wife having an affair? What is she concealing from him? It isn't until the last scene in the movie that we get a clear picture of what his wife was trying to accomplish and how she tried to protect him.

Make sure you have the entire story planned out before starting to write. By having the big picture mapped out, you can then show the viewer a small portion of the entire story. Going back to *The Constant Gardener,* we see snippets of what is going on, but we aren't shown the whole reality. It's as if the scenes are cut short on purpose to nudge us in one direction. We believe that the wife is unfaithful because there is a great deal of conjecture and innuendo.

We catch one glimpse of this sleight of hand when we see her breast feeding a native African baby. We know she was pregnant, and assumed her Caucasian husband is the father. However, we also know that she has been spending a great deal of time with a Kenyan native. By the end of the scene, we realize that she had a miscarriage, but since she was lactating she was feeding babies at an orphanage. It's a great twist and subtly lets us know that all is not what is seems.

The entire architecture behind *The Sixth Sense* is to lead the audience one way, then pull back the curtain to reveal what is really happening. It's like a magician showing you how they perform a card trick. In non-linear movies, the time shifting confuses the audience on one hand, and stacks information together to force us to a conclusion, one that may be inaccurate.

While it does take a great deal of finesse, attention to detail and the intuition of a magician to craft these types of movies, writing one to be clever isn't enough. As we discussed earlier, you can't take a script that could be effectively told chronologically, smash it like it were peanut brittle, then reassemble it out of order and call it a solid film.

Unfortunately, the majority of contest submissions in this category read like a script that was reordered to prove that the writer is very clever. Don't waste your time writing in this manner. As a judge, I will only lose a couple hours of my life reading it before I pass on it. How much time will you have lost?

An example of a poorly executed film told in the non-linear narrative is *Before the Devil Knows You're Dead (2007)*. This film could've been told in a linear fashion, perhaps with one or two flashbacks, and the character exposition and payoff at the end would've been intact. This movie seemed rather gimmicky in its method of storytelling. It tried to be clever, and it fell short.

When creating a screenplay, this method of storytelling can actually detract from your writing. If you submit a non-linear screenplay, as a judge I will assume that you know exactly what you are doing, and you won't get extra points for your attempt to master it. Same goes for a singing contest. If you try to sing "Bohemian Rhapsody," then you better hit every note flawlessly. If your voice doesn't have the range, then stick to Johnny Cash. It's better to tell a simple story well, then a complex one poorly.

Sean Hinchey

HIGH CONCEPT

The High Concept idea is to other genres what a neon light is to a cardboard sign. While writing this genre may seem like a cheap gag to try to get a contest judge to really like your script, look at it from a different angle. A contest judge will have an idea of what your story is about before they even get to page ten.

Usually, High Concept scripts are tied into the Action genre. It's a term you've probably heard before, but what is it? It's any idea that can be briefly explained in a few sentences and the listener will have a full understanding of what the story is about. Sometimes, even one sentence will suffice. What you are doing is tapping into the movie-going experiences of the other party. Later on, I'll be talking about the "A meets B" method of describing a High Concept idea.

The movie *Speed* (1994) is a perfect example of a High Concept script. As a contest judge, I'm always looking over a mountain of scripts. Imagine it's late in the day and I've been reading an enormous amount of material, but nothing has really struck me as being the next contest winner or even a finalist. Before the day is over, I want to get through at least one more script so I can stay on top of the reading process.

I flip through the title pages of several scripts in my mountain of paper and come across one called "Speed." Right away, the title tells me something about what the story will be about. The pacing, mostly likely, will be very fast. As I read the first ten pages of the script, I realize that there is a terrorist bomber who is able to rig his explosives anywhere. The first one is in an elevator. A hot-shot member of the SWAT team rescues the passengers

Write It to Win It!

before they die. In very short order, I learn that a bus is rigged with explosives to detonate if the bus goes below 55 miles per hour. And there it is: the High Concept idea in that final sentence. If you were pitching the script, that's what you would use.

The opening scene establishes the pacing, excitement, and the stakes in this script. The title, as it relates to what the story is about, comes into focus very quickly. A connection to other movies is made clear: it's *Die Hard* (1988) on a bus. This is the "A meets B" method I mentioned earlier. Take something familiar and build upon it. This script has now completely captured my attention. The pages cannot be flipped fast enough and by the time I reach the end, I'm exhausted but rewarded.

This is the reaction that most people get when they read a High Concept screenplay. They are not easy to imagine and can be difficult to write. With a High Concept idea comes a high expectation to deliver. *Speed* could've been a complete flop if the characters weren't developed, the scenes went on for too long, or the the dialogue fell flat.

Some examples of High Concept movies: *Jurassic Park* (1993) is about a man building an amusement park based around genetically grown dinosaurs. *Armored* (2009) is about a group of men who plan to rob the armored car company they work for. *Backdraft* (1991) is about a group of firefighters trying to find a serial arsonist.

All of these High Concept pitches give you a glimpse into what the story will be about. Your mind is able to fill in any blanks. A story about a dinosaur amusement park? There must be people running from the creatures or trying to outsmart them. A High Concept script draws your reader into the story immediately.

Sean Hinchey

There are potential downfalls to writing a High Concept script. The idea of submitting a strong idea can be a bit too on-the-nose. There are judges out there who enjoy reading a well thought out, slower paced story. A High Concept story can come across as a bit too loud or too flashy. Either you will hit or miss with it. This shouldn't stop you from writing such a High Concept script if you have a solid idea, since there are many judges who don't like the smaller, art-house type of stories. You will always be taking a risk with whatever genre you write. Keep in mind, if you try to go big with the High Concept, you better deliver the goods. If you're all frosting and no cake, your script will go nowhere.

Coming up with a High Concept idea is difficult. The key to developing one is to find something that has been done before- the "A meets B" method-and you put a new twist on it. Going back to the example of *Speed* as *Die Hard* on a bus, borrowing from *Die Hard* (1988) has been done many times.

Sudden Death (1995): *Die Hard* in a hockey arena. *Striking Distance* (1993): *Die Hard* on a river. *Passenger 57* (1992): *Die Hard* on plane. Each time, the scripts have generated interest because of their play on a familiar theme. Michael Crichton's *Jurassic Park* is based on the formula and theme from his earlier film *Westworld* (1973).

If the concept works, then it works. There is absolutely nothing wrong with borrowing a previous concept and making it your own. Except in one specific instance: Never use any specific material that you don't own the rights to. I have read many scripts that are High Concept but are based on comic book heroes or other established franchises. One was a James Bond script, which could never be made into a movie unless the rights were secured from the franchise owners. That is highly unlikely. Instead of naming the character "James Bond," create a new name.

Another reason for not using existing characters that you don't own the rights to is that it shows a lack of imagination on the part of the writer. Most people would have no problem coming up with a "Batman" film, or a story based around Tom Clancy's character, Jack Ryan. The groundwork has already been established, so it's easy to build upon that platform.

A judge won't shoot down a script simply because of the rights issue, but some screenplay contests stipulate that you cannot use copyrighted material you are not entitled to. If you're spending time writing a screenplay, do you really want to write something that you won't be able to shop around to production companies?

When writing a High Concept script, keep the story moving forward. There is a fine line between developing the characters too much or too little. While in other genres, it's the character arc that we want to see against the background of the script, in High Concept, the concept is king.

In High Concept stories, we don't need to know too much about the protagonist's background, unless it directly relates to the story. In *Die Hard*, we know that the main character is a police officer visiting his estranged wife and their kids. As the movie progresses, we learn just how resourceful he is. In a different movie, we may need to learn more about that same character. How hard is he working on his marriage? What is his relationship with his kids? None of this matters in the context of the High

Sean Hinchey

Concept story. What does matter is the pacing of the story from beginning to end.

This may sound easy, but High Concept scripts can be very difficult to execute. You have to keep the story moving forward by maintaining the concept of the story. *Speed* is about a bus that will explode if it drops below 55 miles per hour. How do you keep that pace going for almost two hours?

Set the story in a city where going at that speed would be difficult. If the bus were on I-90 in Montana, that would make for a boring story. So, you set the bus in the congestion capital of the world, Los Angeles. You have it drive through construction sites, maneuver around traffic jams and have one of the passengers take over the driving. Through all this, you have a man from the SWAT team try to get on the bus so he can rescue the passengers.

Once you start writing a High Concept script, it's a juggling act: you have to keep all of the balls in the air. If you can maintain the tension from beginning to end, you will have a wildly successful script.

The main problem I've encountered with High Concept scripts is that the story veers away from the concept that captured my interest in the first place. What started out as a compelling idea became a different story. The characters went after something other than what they started with. Don't use a bait and switch technique. Stick with the concept that got the script off the ground and run with it.

It may not be easy, but if you keep it simple and streamlined, it'll be a fun project to write and a compelling story for the contest judges to read. Not only will you have a solid chance at winning a screenwriting contest, but you may also find that your script gets caught up in a bidding war.

KEY POINTS

- You need to be clear what the theme is for your screenplay without making it too complicated. Likewise, be clear what genre of script you are writing and figure out which genre(s) is/are your strong suit.

- When writing a Drama, define what kind of Drama it is a little more specifically. Because there is so much real-world material to draw upon, a Drama has to be great.

- Comedies need to be funny, in terms of the writing. It's not all about physical comedy. And conflict is just as important in a Comedy as it is in any other genre.

- Sci-Fi is about a universal theme told in a different setting. Never get too caught up in the Sci-Fi world at the expense of great storytelling.

- Great Horror shouldn't be confused with copious amounts of gore.

- Suspense and tension play to the theater of the mind, which makes for better storytelling than anything you can actually show the audience.

- Period Piece screenplays aren't an excuse for heavy description. While historical accuracy is fine, a few liberties can be taken for the sake of good storytelling.

- Westerns are usually stories about revenge, which

means there needs to be a great villain. Because Westerns take place in an earlier time, it's acceptable to have a slower pace in your storytelling.

- Everybody loves a great Thriller.

- Be careful how far you push your protagonist back; at some point they need to spring back in a logical fashion.

- Family movies need to be about one thing, and only one thing. If there isn't a major sacrifice on behalf of the protagonist, a Family story won't work.

- Non-Linear stories are used to create tension that cannot be effectively accomplished in any other method of story-telling. If there isn't tension in every scene, then the Non-Linear format will come across as a gimmick.

- High Concept: you know it when you see it. While they are hard to conceive of, High Concept stories are even harder to write. The expectations are sky-high.

Sean Hinchey

SEVEN: DETAILS

A GREAT TITLE

Do you have a great title to your script? Is it something that helps sell it? There are movies that I've seen where the title alone pushes my desire to see it. Granted, most people saw *The Empire Strikes Back* (1980) because it was the second "Star Wars" movie to come out. But even on its own, it's such a powerful title. "Empire" conjures up images of a far reaching entity. "Strikes Back" means that it is payback time. Even before I saw this film, I knew the tone would be dark.

A movie title needs to suggest something about what the film will be about, yet it needs to keep you guessing just enough to want to see it. Titles should be good teases.

Using people's names can be a risky move for a movie title, unless they are well known, iconic or historical people. For example, the documentary *Marilyn* (1963) would have most people correctly guessing that it's about Marilyn Monroe. That would be effective for a feature film based on her life.

However, titles such as *Erin Brockovich* (2000) had me guessing what the film would be about. Julia Roberts' star power made this a moot point in terms of the success of this film. *Michael Clayton* (2007) went by the name *Fixer* in Japan, which is a much cooler title.

Aside from the names of people you may or may not know, there are other screenplay titles that just don't work. How does a writer pick a great title? A title should encapsulate what the story is about. If you are writing a heist movie, can you incorporate some variation of the word "heist" into the title? How about "steal," "theft," or "robbery"? If it's an impossible job where the odds are against the crew about to pull of the heist, you could use something along the lines of "The Goliath Job." The point here is that if you have two people who are going to be trying to steal something valuable, you wouldn't want to use their names. It tells the contest judge nothing about what your story is about.

You could even do a word play on other types of movies. *An American Werewolf in London (1981)* is a play on similar types of the old school B-Horror Movies. It also gives you a good idea who the main character is-or will turn into-and where the story takes place.

Go with the first title that comes to mind. Usually, when I am developing an idea for a script, the title comes rather quickly. If I'm having trouble, I tweak it slightly so that it sounds concise and logical. If you are still having trouble coming up with a title, then do this quick exercise. Write down on a piece of paper the first ten or so words that come to mind when you think of your script. They could be locations the story takes place in, emotions, or even physical items in the story. Don't spend too much time thinking; just go with your instinct. Take the words that you feel best describe your story and see if you can arrange them into a compelling title.

There should be a moment in the script where the title becomes clear. It could be something somebody says or maybe it encapsulates the tone of the film. *Inception (2010)* sounds cool, but there is also a moment in the film where we realize that the protagonist is talking about creating an idea in someone's mind in such a manner that they believe they created it themselves: the moment of inception.

Sean Hinchey

Wages of Fear (1953) gives you an idea of what the story is about. Two teams have to deliver very unstable nitroglycerine to an oil fire in the South America. This story was remade as *Sorcerer (1977)*. Both movies are well done, but the original title, which is the same title as the novel it's based on, packs more punch. The novel (and film) *I Am Legend (2007)* has a nice ring to it, but for me, the original film *The Omega Man (1971)* sounds even better.

Think of the movie poster. It may sound like an ego trip, but this can be a big help. What will the font look like? Will the words dominate the whole page or be underneath pictures of the main characters? Visualizing the structure of the words on the page allows you to see how the story would be presented in terms of advertising. Would it draw people in? Would it be too verbose? What would people think when that saw that title during the movie previews?

The reason why this is more of an exercise than just wishful thinking is this approach is similar to the way others will process your screenplay. The title is part of the entire package, the first impression that people have about your script. Many contest-submitted scripts have absolutely horrible titles.

While the title of your script won't necessarily make or break your chance of winning a contest, a great one is easy to remember. No contest judge has ever said, "I just read the greatest script ever but I forgot what it's called." When you are getting feedback on your screenplay, you should ask that person what they think of the title. If they hesitate or try to downplay their answer, you may want to come up with a new one. Make it catchy, concise, and memorable.

ICONIC MOMENT

Does your screenplay have an Iconic moment in it? It's that one scene that summarizes your story. If you are able to craft a moment that hooks the contest judge into your story, chances are it will stick with them when they are deciding the winners.

What do we mean when we talk about these memorable moments? Sometimes these moments are at the end of a film, a great closing that brands that story into your mind. Think of Keyser Soze in *The Usual Suspect (1995)*. When the main character is revealed to be the monster that everyone was looking for, it warps the viewer's mind. The famous "Luke, I am your father" line from *The Empire Strikes Back (1980)* changes the entire course of the hero's journey. Just consider a few Iconic Moments: the car chase in *Bullit (1968)*, Indiana Jones shooting the swordsman in *Raiders of the Lost Ark (1981)*, "Mrs. Robinson, you're trying to seduce me!" from *The Graduate (1967)* and "Rosebud" from *Citizen Kane (1941)*. When you talk to your friends or fellow writers and say, "We go to the mattresses," they know you're talking about *The Godfather (1972)*.

Reflect on some of your favorite movies. What was that one scene or snippet of dialogue that you remember? We're talking about that one flash in your mind, especially if you haven't seen the film in years. You are looking for something very simple here.

For example, in *Unforgiven (1992)*, the main character finds out that his best friend was brutally murdered by the sheriff. He then takes a couple huge swigs off a liquor bottle. The movie is filled with some incredible dialogue; many scenes pop into my head because of the way they are written, acted, and directed. However, that one scene is iconic because everything the protagonist has struggled against is about to come back. It's as if he's drinking in all the evil and is about to unleash hell.

Chinatown (1974) has that great final moment: "Forget about it, Jake. It's Chinatown." However, the scene where Jake gets his nose cut by one of the enforcers (played by the director, Roman Polanski) is a very powerful scene. It shows just how serious the entire situation is.

The Producers (1968) has a down-on-his-luck producer cleaning his grimy window with cold coffee and a silk tie as he stares at a Rolls Royce across the street. He then yells, "Flaunt it baby, flaunt it!" *Mississippi Burning (1988)* has a pivotal scene where an FBI agent walks into a barbershop where a corrupt police officer is getting a shave. The agent takes the razor from the barber and calmly shaves the fear-stricken officer while the agent talks.

The list can just keep going on and on. Make up your own list. Again, what you are looking for is that piece of the film that really encapsulates what the story is about. If somebody hadn't watched that movie, what would you show them to give them an idea of what it's about?

Now that you've figured out what makes some of your favorite movies work, see if you have a similar scene or piece of dialogue that sums up your screenplay. It could just need a little bit of work to make it truly memorable. This is important: you're not necessarily looking for a catchphrase. While this could be what you end up with, don't focus on writing one clever or cool sentence. Here's why.

"I'll be back!", "Do you feel lucky punk?", "Show me the money!" and "I'm mad as hell, and I'm not going to take it anymore!" are all phrases that have made it into our culture. Did the writers know at the time that they were crafting words that would go beyond the film itself? Most likely not.

If you are trying to craft something memorable about your screenplay that results in a one line sentence, it may not work out as planned. There could be other lines that writers have inserted into their screenplays which they thought would catch on but went nowhere. Don't put too much emphasis only on the line of dialogue. If you are trying to craft a clever sentence, make sure it is properly utilized in the right context.

For example, the line from *The Terminator* (1984)— "I'll be back"—works for several reasons. Arnold Schwarzenegger delivers it deadpan, where another actor may not have pulled it off. Also, had he not said the line and instead pulled out a gun and started shooting, the scene wouldn't have had as much of an impact. However, he leaves the building, drives a car in through the front door, *then* starts shooting. His line is followed by something unexpected. It's called the hook.

You are trying to craft something that catches the audience off guard and makes it memorable. That's something to keep in mind as you put your words down on paper. A college professor for one of my journalism classes had us quickly write an article based on a bunch of facts he threw out at us. It was a fictional situation based on a man robbing a pizza parlor and doubling back to take a calzone with him in the getaway car. For some reason I worked that information into the article.

Sean Hinchey

When he was grading the papers, he awarded the people who used the bit about the calzone the highest grades. Why? Because it was an oddity. When you hear that a man has the cash in his hand but goes back to grab a free dinner, it makes you pause for a moment. Obviously, the hook worked because I remember that story after all these years.

Except for the calzone example, everything else so far has been based on an existing film. What you have are visual examples of iconic moments. How do you craft a moment on paper so that you can allow the contest judge to see your hook?

Let's start with what you know. You've thought about your favorite films and have decided on which moments in those films are iconic for you. You recognize that for your script, the iconic moment has to be about a great line in a great scene that summarizes your script. Think along the lines of a man sitting at a breakfast table in knight's armor because he works at a King Arthur dinner theater, as he suffers the barb of "He's just a fast-food knight," from Garden State (2004).

As you write (or re-write) your screenplay, look at the dialogue in relation to the scene that it's in. Create an exchange that only makes sense in that moment. It's a slice of time that says, "You had to be there."

Every script that I have pushed into the finalist round or as a contest winner has had at least one iconic moment that really dazzled me. If you work on each scene as if that were the only one the contest judge was going to read, then you would be creating one great moment after another. Layer in a hook into each of your scenes; you never know which one will stick. It's not about trying to be clever, it's about quality writing that will get you noticed by the contest judge.

Sean Hinchey

THE NOTES WILL TELL ME WHY I LOST

In talking to different writers submitting their screenplays to talent agencies, production companies, and screenwriting contests, I've noticed a common myth that needs to be debunked. In most cases, you will not receive coverage reports or notes on why your script didn't win the contest or receive consideration from an agency.

There are several reasons why it's unlikely you will get this information. First, you don't actually have a right to those details. Many contests even explain this in their submission forms. There's a good reason for this. When you submit an entry fee for a contest, the money goes to pay the contest judges, advertising costs, and cash awards for the contest winners. You are not paying for a coverage report.

If the contest generated coverage reports for every script submitted, it would take months to process all of that information. When you enter a contest, you are competing for a prize. If you want to get feedback through a coverage report, those services are available through a variety of sources.

Many writers confuse the true purpose of a contest. Much of this seems to come from TV shows such as *American Idol* where the judges give immediate, but brief, feedback to the contestant. Therefore, many writers feel that they are owed a reason for not winning the contest.

Understand that there is nothing for the company running the contest to gain by giving you the notes on your script. Contest judges submit abbreviated reports to the people who run the contest. Usually, it's a brief rating grid regarding the various components of the screenplay, a synopsis and a few sentences regarding the pros and cons of the material. Usually, the judge explains in the cons why they didn't move the script forward to the next round.

If the contest released all of these notes, imagine the backlash they would receive from the disgruntled writers. I've received plenty of emails regarding coverage reports-a paid critique-that I've done on scripts. Most of the time, they want further justification for the shortcomings of their scripts. I find this odd, since my coverage reports detail the strengths and weaknesses of their material.

How much information do you need about why a scene needs to be tweaked or a character further developed? Multiply that by the number of contest submissions in every contest, and the entire process would come to a grinding halt. Again, the purpose of the contest is to find the diamond in the rough, not give everyone who wasn't a finalist a reason why they didn't make the cut. Because you wouldn't be getting the complete picture of the pros and cons regarding your script, you may get the wrong impression of how the judge perceived your script.

For example, I generally write three major points for the positive elements in the script and three for the negative ones. Generally, there is a great deal more that I can write about the pros and cons. However, I pick the most salient ones that cover a broad cross-section of the script. This is done for brevity and because I have hundreds of scripts to read.

As the writer of your material, if you were to read the reports, you may think that the contest judge didn't understand the whole story because they left out a lot of information in the brief report. While that may be your perception, it's far from the reality. Because this could cause misconceptions and headaches for the contest organizers, you usually won't receive any coverage reports.

If you want feedback on your script, use a coverage service. They offer different levels of coverage tailored to your needs and many of them have one-on-one phone consultations which can be very beneficial. If you have writer friends, read each other's scripts and offer your own feedback in exchange for theirs. The contests that do offer a critique give you extra value for your dollar. It may be worth seeking out those contests so that even if you don't win, you'll at least get a coverage report on your script.

The reality is, you may never know why you lost in a particular screenwriting competition. It's possible that you could resubmit your script in another contest and become a finalist or even win. Judging is a subjective situation. Each judge has different tastes and expectations. It's important not to take it personally because the judge's job is to pick the best one. Just because your material doesn't win nor even make it as a finalist doesn't mean your writing is horrible.

REPETITION IS REDUNDANT

As a screenwriter, you need to find a balance between getting your point across and repeating yourself too many times. While you may want to make sure that the contest judge reading your script understands a key element in your screenplay, beating them over the head with the same element comes across as amateurish.

What contest writers need to understand is that judges have read hundreds of screenplays. There is very little that gets past their purview. As a writer, it's natural to feel the need to have a contest judge "get" an important detail in your story. How do you reveal something so that you know the contest judges don't miss your point?

Make your point once and only once. Why is this important? You don't have time in your screenplay to go over the same material several different ways. The story needs to move forward, characters need to be developed, and the conflict explored to its ultimate end. If the same information is hammered home again and again, story development stagnates. Repetition of a key point is like stopping and reversing yourself. Once the forward momentum is lost, it's difficult to get back up to speed.

Echoing information that has been revealed is insulting to the contest judge. While this may not be your intent, that's how it comes across. We've all been in conversations where somebody explains something to the point that it's been beaten into the ground. If I were to make endless analogies about this point, I would be insulting you, the reader of this book, because I would assume that you haven't quite gotten my point. Just as I have to trust that you are intelligent enough to understand the gist of what

I'm saying, you need to have faith in the contest judges.

However, if you do explain the same point again, it needs to be built upon, giving the reader new information. For example, let's say a couple of co-workers are talking about their reluctance to attend a company holiday party. If you bring this up again in your story, add something the reader doesn't know. Maybe there is some silly game the boss insists that everyone plays that is a bit humiliating, or perhaps there will be someone in attendance neither of them likes.

By doing this enhancement, you are enriching the story because we are seeing the different layers of the story. In the film *Inception (2010)* we hear about the main character's ex-wife. However, each time she is discussed, there is a new tidbit of information revealed.

Finally, recognize who your audience is when you give out information. You may explain something three times to three different people **in the story**, but you are really telling the reader the same information three different times. Who needs to know this information, the characters or the reader?

Let's use as an example a detective story. The first detective who arrives on the scene examines a dead body and speculates about how the victim was killed. Back at the police station, the supervisor would want to know how the victim was killed. For the sake of the reader, the detective isn't going to repeat exactly the same information that we heard in the prior scene.

Instead, he may reveal the clues found on the body, but then quickly change the subject to talk about who that victim was to see if there was a motive. As the detective goes to the morgue to speak to the medical examiner, the reader will gain more information about the circumstances of the event.

In real life, the detective would probably repeat the exact same information to his boss and the medical examiner. Why? Because everyone would need to be up to speed on the current data. In a screenplay, information is exchanged for the benefit of the *reader*, not to assist the *characters*.

This type of information exchange is evident in franchise movies. For example, in the "James Bond" films each movie reintroduces the character in a different way. This is so that the people who have never seen James Bond will get to know his character. For the audience members who are fanatical followers-such as myself-the characteristics of Bond are altered so that the same tidbits aren't repeated in each movie. *The Simpsons Movie* (2007) accomplished this in their first motion picture to date. They used a new angle to reveal the wacky family to the first-time audience so it wouldn't be a rehash to the devoted fans.

Believe that your writing capabilities will get your major points across concisely, without leaving anything important out. Also, trust that the contest judges with their years of experience aren't going to miss anything important. A great script will speak for itself without the need to constantly hammer home the same points.

Sean Hinchey

AVOID THE ORDINARY

There are a few overused items that should be avoided in your screenplay. On their own, none of these potential pitfalls warrant their own section, so they are compiled here into one neat little portion of this book. If you use all of these improperly, the odds are that your script will not advance in a screenwriting competition. They may seem like such trivial matters, but they are not.

It's like this: Try going on a long hike with a grain of sand in your sock and see how far you get.

What is the proper use of these elements in your screenplay? This is the one time in this book that you are on your own. If you don't know how to properly apply them to your material, then perhaps you simply should avoid using them. Generally, don't use movie references in your screenplay. It's an easy way of getting a point across and usually comes across as a smug inside joke.

Sometimes they work in films such as *The Player (1992)*, where the story is about the movie industry. In *You've Got Mail (1998)* the joke about "going to the mattresses" works because it is used briefly. Another *Godfather* reference is used in *The Freshman (1990)* to great success because Marlon Brando is in the film.

However, the risk that a writer runs when using a movie reference is that the reader may not have seen the movie you are alluding to. What has happened is that you are trying to make a connection based on information outside of your control. There is always another way to reveal something pertinent to the story. More important, referring to a specific scene in another movie takes the reader out of your story and makes them realize that they are indeed reading a screenplay. The idea behind a great script is that the audience is transported to another world, one of your creation. The trick is to keep the reader engaged in *your* story. Never break the spell.

You are better served by using other mechanisms to propel the story forward than by referencing another film because it comes across as unimaginative or lazy. When submitting your script for a contest, you need every advantage at your disposal.

In addition to screenplay references, stay away from specific Los Angeles remarks. Until I actually lived on the West Coast, many of the screenwriting nods to the entertainment capital of the world went over my head. Even after living there, I found many of the references too specific to certain areas of town. There was a great deal of this in *Volcano (1997)*.

Not all contest judges live in Los Angeles, so any reference may be lost to them. More important, it comes across as trying to be clever. In previous chapters we've discussed just how far clever will get you in a screenwriting contest. Like the film references, insider references to Los Angeles may come across as lazy or unoriginal. For East Coasters, I'd offer the same caution regarding New York City. You don't want to exclude your audience.

Be wary of the jaded twenty-something protagonist. Few people want to see, or read, a story about a young adult whose outlook on the world is so cynical, yet they somehow have all the answers. Most of the time, these characters come from privileged backgrounds, so their angst comes across as very self-indulgent.

Look at movies that have younger characters who are

truly hard on their luck. Instead of them sitting back and lamenting how unfair the world is, we see them elevating themselves and bettering their lives. The story becomes about them overcoming social obstacles to succeed, rather than wallow in self-pity.

In movies such as *Less Than Zero* (1987) we see how privilege and excess have complicated the characters' lives; the story doesn't glorify being the child of wealthy parents. Instead, it exposes the abuse of great freedom at an age where teens are too immature to harness it properly.

A big problem regarding stories with these apathetic characters is that there are so many people playing this role in reality television. Also, it's hard to develop a quality character who is lamenting his sorrows for an entire script. What kind of growth will the character have? What does he want? But most important, what is his problem?

Shielding the true identity of a character for a dramatic reveal later can be confusing. I've read many submitted screenplays that have a "Shadowy Woman" or "Man One" lurking in the background of the story. Later on, the name changes and they are the long lost brother, an undercover police officer, or a serial murderer. When introducing a significant character, give them a name. You can say in the description something along the lines of, "BOB stands at the entrance to the alley. However, there isn't any light on him, so his identity is concealed for now." That tells the contest judge that this person may come into play later in the story, but he is still a mystery to the characters in the story.

If you are telling a horror story and there is a masked

or cloaked person terrorizing the other characters, then give that character an obvious title—Phantom, Ghost, or Ghoul—something that indicates who this character is without revealing who the person behind the mask is until the end, if you want to keep it a surprise.

Building suspense in a story can be important to the payoff. Be careful how you do it because the judge is trying to formulate the visuals in their head. Make it easy for them to see your world. If they have to go back and read previous pages to figure out what that person was earlier in the script, you may have stunted the momentum.

Many scripts are based around a character who is an utter loser and failure in life. The majority of these stories revolve around a man-rarely a woman—who is still suffering from bullying, acne, humiliation, or some other tragedy from high school. By the end of the script, they are finally able to shed their tormented past and are able to keep their head held up high. Up to this point, everything seems reasonable. Here's the kicker: that person then comes out with a best-selling book about their life, and at a book signing, they meet the person of their dreams.

Unless the story is about a person who is struggling to write a book, this device is very *deus ex machina*; it's a contrived ending. Out of all the scripts that I've read, the main character never has even the slightest hint of having the writing bug. Yet, in one single final scene we are supposed to believe that our main character suddenly wrote a book, found a publisher, and is now a world-class author who has it all?

Look to a film such as *Night Shift (1982)*. Can't it be enough that a character dumps his neurotic fiancée, stands up to his bullying delivery man, and tries to develop a relationship with a woman he's fallen in love with? The resolution at the end of the story has to be in relation to what the person is trying to achieve, to his want. If the protagonist has never attempted to write a book, a song, develop the next great computer application, or cure a disease, then don't have the main character accomplish this as some type of "in your face" moment at the end. It simply doesn't work, it's hackneyed and amateurish. Don't do it.

I've discussed the point about keeping your description lean in another chapter, but it's worth reiterating: don't get lazy. Never write anything that's too concise for something big and important in your story. For example, I've seen several scripts that have a car chase where the description has been similar to: "Standard car chase through the city streets. The bad guy gets away leaving the good guy fuming." While we don't need to see every single detail about the car chase, you need to provide enough description to engage us in the sequence. Add something to the scene to make it original. You need to own your scene.

Writing something so basic begs the question, if you're too lazy to write out the high points of the chase, then why should I have the energy to read it? Also, if you choose to reduce an involved sequence to a sentence or two, then you are admitting that it's probably a dull, unoriginal scene.

Go easy on the camera descriptions. That is to say, don't direct the screenplay—write it. ANGLE ON, SNAP ZOOM, DOLLY LEFT: these are all decisions that would be made by the director. Having in-depth camera movement slows down the read of the story. If the contest judge reads such a description, they are going to assume that is has significance.

For example, if a man is about to go for a walk in the desert, you may have in the description:

ANGLE ON: The cellphone underneath the front seat.

This tells the reader that something significant may happen. He left his cell phone in the car, probably by accident. This could be a turning point in the story. Maybe he'll get lost and have no way of calling for help. However, if you are filling the script with camera angles because you feel that the story has to unfold in a specific manner, you are hurting yourself. After a few pages they will be an annoyance, not a guide, to your storytelling.

Again, you may shrug off all of these seemingly minor points. However, they are nuisances that can add up to a significant number of negative points that may affect your chances of advancing in a contest. This is especially true if the judge reads a script after yours that has avoided all of these pitfalls.

KEY POINTS

- A great title helps the reader get a sense of what your story is about. Using the name of a character for the title usually isn't a good idea unless that person is well known.

- You should have at least one moment in your script that really dazzles the judge and summarizes the entire screenplay. The iconic moment isn't just about having great dialogue; it needs to be everything about that scene.

- Never expect to receive notes to tell you why your script didn't win a contest. Use professional coverage services or get feedback from friends before you enter a contest.

- If you ram home a key point again and again in your screenplay, you are suggesting that the judge isn't smart enough to understand what you are saying.

- There are ways to reveal important points through different methods, so reveal key information over the course of the entire script.

- Insider references to a specific city or industry will make the reader feel like an outsider and they won't be able to engage in your story.

- Minor snags in your story may seem like no big deal, but if you have too many of them they add up, and your story won't advance further in the contest.

EIGHT: THE BIG QUESTION

CAN YOUR SCRIPT BE PRODUCED?

It's time to wrap up this book and see if we can bring all these points together so you can stop reading and get back to writing. When we started on this journey, I brought up the question of you being prepared to win. Hopefully, that created the proper mindset for the entire book. We are going to revisit that issue, now that you are armed with an array of tools to polish up your next script.

The big questions you need to ask yourself as you move forward in your writing is: Are you working on a screenplay that can be brought to life on the big screen? Does your material have what it takes to bring actors, directors, and producers together to turn your paper world into a real life film?

Throughout the book, I've emphasized that a contest judge looks at a screenplay as a potentially viable product to be turned into a movie. If we can't visualize it on the big screen, it won't win. Simple as that. So far we've dissected structure, different types of characters, dialogue, description-I don't need to tell you, because you've been reading it.

This is what it all comes down to: crafting a screenplay that can actually be made. It's not enough to write a great script, you need to make one that can be produced.

Keep up on what movies are doing well at the box office. There are always trends that come and go, and this isn't to say that you have to write the screenplay that rides those coattails. However, if you are working on a film that may be difficult to cast but you have an unfinished vampire film and you know that production companies are looking for that genre, then your decision is fairly clear.

How do you go about finding what the movie industry wants? There are many screenwriting websites that offer information on box office receipts, recent script sales, and up-and-coming writers. With the internet, you have access to a great deal of data that would've been hard to find even ten years ago.

Start digging and gathering information to figure out what the pulse of the industry is. However, you should always be writing what you are most comfortable with. To go back to the earlier example, you may submit your vampire script only to find that the industry has suddenly gone cold on that genre. Producers are very fickle people. But, you have to have some information to use as a starting point.

To circle back around to the main gist of this chapter, write the script that can be produced. I've seen lots of screenwriting submissions where the writing is good. They have well-developed characters, an interesting plot, and the dialogue is decent. However, the script wasn't something that could be produced, that certain dose of magic to make it a motion picture-worthy screenplay.

It's like watching a music competition on TV. You see a lot of talent but there's not enough going for them to win an album recording contract. They get close, but they don't have enough to get them over the final hurdle and close the deal.

In the ten plus years that I've been reading screenplays,

I've had writers ask me a variety of questions: "Is the writing good?", "Did you like my characters?", "Do you think it could win a contest?", "Do you think a production company would read it?", "If you were doing a coverage report would you give it a recommend or at least a consider?"

They are ignoring the most important question, the one way of looking at the whole industry that could change your perception of writing: "Do you see my screenplay as a motion picture?"

Think about that for one minute. Here is a question so basic, yet so bold. All of the other questions touch the periphery of this grand prize. If someone answered all of the other questions to your satisfaction, yet you never asked this question of yourself, then you are missing the whole point of writing.

This is what writing screenplays all comes down to. Contests are stepping stones to something bigger and better. In football, the quarterback doesn't throw the football to where his receiver is. He throws it to the spot where the receiver will be.

You've read this entire book, hopefully. You have a solid understanding of how all the parts of a screenplay should fit together. At the very least you recognize the pitfalls that maybe you've fallen into when you've been writing. Now, you can to take all of that information and write a screenplay that will win a screenwriting contest. But, you need to look beyond that, to where the football will be thrown. You need to write the script that can be sold, produced, and turned into a movie.

If you write your next script with a focus on getting it

Sean Hinchey

made into a movie, you will have a better chance of winning a contest than those who are out to simply win the contest. That's the type of script I would love to read.

Best of luck to all of you in your present and future screenwriting adventures!

Write It to Win It!

ACKNOWLEDGMENTS

My wife Lana has been a huge inspiration in my life. I never would've been able to finish this book if she wasn't supportive of me locking myself away in the office to toil away at all hours. Always one of my most honest critics when it comes to my writing, and my biggest advocate, I can never thank her enough.

Chris Lockhart, who has been a mentor, devil's advocate and great friend, thank you. His aggravating advice has always pushed me to do better. Special thanks to Donzi for everything you've done.

My Mom took me on some of the most wonderful international adventures, allowing me to experience a wide array of cultures that opened my mind to infinite possibilities. Thank you for so much. And thanks to my Dad who taught me what he knew, and found others to instruct me in what he didn't. Miss you every day.

Thanks to the folks at Havenhurst Books: Steve Rohr for *finally* agreeing to publish my book, Chris Freeman, for his magical editing skills, and Leo Baligaya for his work on the book layout and cover.

Thanks to Marvin Acuna for helping me launch my weekly blog about screenwriting for contests. To Shelly Mellot and Misse Geatty over at *Script* Magazine, for allowing me to read for their contests over the years. They are some of the kindest people I've ever worked with. And thanks to the old gang from ICM who have scattered to the winds to develop their own empires.

SUGGESTED READING & RESOURCES

Before I leave you, I wanted to make a few other suggestions of resources that might help you be a better writer. By no means is this list exhaustive, but here you are.

As I see it, there are two types of writers who operate at extreme ends of the spectrum, and I strongly urge you not to fall into either of these categories. First are the writers who are so sure of their abilities that they feel no need to do anything other than write. Please understand that reading a book about writing or taking a workshop is not about questioning an individual's writing prowess. It's about honing the skills you have, strengthening any problem areas, and perhaps discovering ways to enhance your project that you may never have considered.

The second type of writer is the one who buys every single book about writing. If there's a writing workshop or course to be enrolled in, they've done it. These are the writers who are well versed in the theories of screenwriting, but they've actually generated very little material. The best way to learn about writing is by doing it. Don't get caught up in the perpetual preparation to write. Find a balance, because at some point, you need to sit down and do it if you want to win a screenwriting contest.

These are some books you might find helpful:

- Marc Norman's *What Happens Next?* talks about writing, screenwriters, and Hollywood as an industry.

- Thomas Pope's *Good Scripts, Bad Scripts* analyzes a great cross- section of screenplays.

Sean Hinchey

- Syd Field's *Screenplay: The Foundations of Screenwriting* covers the fundamentals of writing a screenplay.

- Blake Snyder's *Save the Cat! The Last Book on Screenwriting You'll Ever Need* offers some great insight into the writing process.

And here are a few websites of interest:

- TwoAdverbs.com has some great articles, interviews, and other relevant resources. There's a link to *The Inside Pitch Blog* that is written by a Hollywood Insider.

- DoneDealPro.com has an exhaustive list of screenplay contests, script sales, and interviews. Some of the information is free, while other sections require an annual membership.

- KoldCast.tv has some incredible, original web-based programming. Much can be learned from telling a story in five- to ten-minute formats.

- Wordplayer.com is operated by two writers with a long list of film credits. The site has produced scripts for you to read, and it includes a forum and some informative columns.

- ScreenwritingExpert.com is my own weekly blog, offering tips about writing for screenplay contests.

Courses such as these can also be worthwhile:

- Steven Wolfson at UCLA offers some fantastic semester-long courses in screenwriting. I have taken a few of his weekend workshops, which forced me to rethink my entire writing process.

- Marc Zicree offers a great mentoring workshop that is accessible even if you don't live in Los Angeles. www.zicree.com

- Michael Hauge travels through the country to give his weekend workshops. I found him to be a good speaker. When I took the course, he spent the second day showing us a feature film so we could discuss it in class. That was not an effective use of time in my opinion. However, he may have changed the format and in any case he offers some valuable material.

Script Services:

I realize this is a shameless plug, but I perform personalized script consultations at www.screenwritingexpert.com. When I worked in the story department at ICM, we'd trade scripts so we could give each other feedback. As a result, I personally have never had to use any script services. There are a lots of script consultation companies out there. If you decide to use one, just be sure that you are dealing with an experienced reading staff. I've heard rumors of certain companies using unpaid college interns to perform the reads in exchange for college credit. The turnover rate among readers would be high, so the readers wouldn't gain a vast reservoir of reading skills, which would suggest to me that you wouldn't get a great value for your money.

ABOUT THE AUTHOR

Sean Hinchey earned his Bachelor's Degree in Broadcast Journalism from the Boston University, School of Communications. His work as a story editor for ICM and as a judge for many prestigious contests, such as the Big Break has made him a sought after script consultant. He is the author of the award-winning book, *Backpacking Through Divorce*. His creation, the original web series Dirty Bomb Diaries, reached two million internet hits and was made on a $600 budget. His blog, which can be found at www.screenwritingexpert.com, offers tips on writing for a screenplay contest.

www.ingramcontent.com/pod-product-compliance
Lightning Source LLC
Chambersburg PA
CBHW071712160426
43195CB00012B/1659